Francis Orpen Morris

**Records of Animal Sagacity and Character**

With a Preface on the Future Existence of the Animal Creation

TO

# THE HONOURABLE ANNE EMMA CAVENDISH,

## THE FOLLOWING PAGES

ARE

BY HER PERMISSION

### Inscribed

BY HER OBLIGED AND OBEDIENT SERVANT

## THE AUTHOR.

# CONTENTS

# PREFACE.

It would seem hardly possible that animals could be ill-used by
any persons who believed in the possibility, if not the probability, of their future existence. Most people give no thought
to this subject. The idea of such a thing has probably never
occurred to their minds; and if suggested to them, many would
no doubt deny the possibility, and many more the probability,
of a future resurrection or restoration of the animal creation.

I will first shew that there is nothing irrational in the
notion, inasmuch as it has been held by men, the greatness of
the mental powers of some of whom, the first-named at all
events, none will deny: and secondly, will bring forward some
of the arguments which may well be supposed to have had
weight with them in forming their opinions on the subject.

Thus wrote the great Bishop Butler, one of the most profound
thinkers that ever lived :—" We cannot argue from the reason
of the thing, that death is the destruction of living agents,
neither can we find any thing throughout the whole analogy
of nature, to afford us even the slightest presumption, that

B

animals ever lose their living powers; much less, if it were
possible, that they lose them by death." And again, observing that "it is thought an insuperable difficulty that they
should be immortal, and by consequence, capable of everlasting happiness," he proceeds to remark, that "even
supposing it were implied, as it is not in the least, in the
natural immortality of brutes, that they must arrive at great
attainments, and become rational and moral agents, even this
would be no difficulty, since we know not what latent powers
they may be endued with.". . . . "But the natural immortality
of brutes does not in the least imply that they are endued with
any latent capacities of a rational or moral nature. And the
economy of the universe might require that there should be
living creatures without any capacities of this kind. And all
difficulties, as to the manner how they are to be disposed of,
are so apparently and wholly founded in our ignorance, that it
is wonderful they should be insisted upon by any but such as
are weak enough to think they are acquainted with the whole
system of things."

So again, in *Tertullian against Hermogenes*, we read :—" Then
will there be an end of death, when the devil, who presides
over it, shall have departed into the fire that God has prepared
for him—when the revelation of the sons of God shall have
redeemed the creation from evil, everywhere subject to vanity,
—when, the innocence and perfectness of the creation being
restored, the cattle shall be in harmony with the wild beasts,
and little children shall play with serpents—when the Father
shall have placed under the feet of the Son his enemies."

Speaking of the above passage, Poole, in his *Synopsis Critic-
orum*, says, "The last part of this extract agrees with the

opinions of the Rabbins, who believe that even dumb animals will obtain a better state when men shall rise. See Manassem on the Resurrection."

And thus also wrote the Rev. John Wesley :—

" They too were immortal. . . . They themselves also shall be delivered, (not by annihilation—annihilation is not deliverance,) from the present 'bondage of corruption,' into a measure of the glorious liberty of the children of God." . . . . " They will be restored, not only to that measure of understanding which they had in Paradise, but to a degree of it as much higher than that, as the understanding of an elephant is beyond that of a worm. And whatever affections they had in the Garden of God, will be restored with vast increase; being exalted and refined in a manner which we ourselves are not now able to comprehend." . . . . " May I be permitted to mention here a conjecture concerning the brute creation ? What, if it should then please the All-wise, the All-gracious Creator, to raise them higher in the scale of beings ? What, if it should please Him, when He made us 'equal to angels,' to make them what we are now,—creatures capable of God ; capable of knowing, and loving, and enjoying, the Author of their being ? If it should be so, ought our eye to be evil because He is good ? However this be, He will certainly do what will be most for his own glory." . . . . " As a recompense for what they once suffered while under the 'bondage of corruption,' when God has ' renewed the face of the earth,' and their corruptible body has put on incorruption, they shall enjoy happiness suited to their state, without alloy, without interruption, and without end." . . . . " Leaving one of these unbounded eras to the Father of Eternity, to whom alone duration without beginning belongs, let us turn out thoughts on duration without end. This is not an incommunicable attribute of the great Creator, but he has been graciously pleased to make innumerable multitudes of his creatures partakers of it. He has imparted this, not only to angels, and archangels, and all the companies of heaven, who are not intended to die, but to glorify Him and live in His presence for ever; but also to the inhabitants of the earth, who dwell in houses of clay. Their bodies, indeed, are *crushed before the moth*, but their souls will never die  God made them, as an ancient writer speaks, to be '*pictures of his own eternity.*' Indeed all spirits, we have reason to believe, are clothed with immortality, having no inward principle of corruption, and being liable to no external violence." . . . " What then is the barrier between men and brutes, the line which they cannot pass? It is not reason. Set aside that ambiguous term; exchange it for the plain word understanding, and who can deny that brutes have this? We may as well deny that they have sight or hearing."

Thus also another writer, the Rev. S. Thompson :—" Certainly existence is better than non-existence, supposing the existence not to be miserable. But the existence of the animals, before the entrance of sin into the world, was not miserable. Therefore if the annihilation of animals take place, then the dispensations of Providence diminish in their improvements, which is impossible." . . . " If the devil has the power of death in this present world, we cannot suppose that he will possess this power in the invisible and eternal world,—nay, this power of the devil has already been diminished by the death of Christ, for Christ came to destroy the works of the

devil,—I say, if the devil was the primary cause of death, and
if the animals will eternally cease to be by annihilation, and
if Christ came to destroy the works of the devil, then some of
these things must follow :—either the devil will hold so much
of his usurped dominion over the animals if they are to be
annihilated, in opposition to Christ who came to destroy his
works, or Christ must be deficient, either in goodness, wisdom,
or power, by which He is not able to rescue the animals
which were the works of His own hands, from the power of
His great adversary. But Christ cannot be deficient, either in
goodness, wisdom, or power; therefore the devil must sink
under His omnipotent arm, and deliver up the prey, the
animals, as the unalienable property of Christ. He is *the
Creator, the Preserver, the Governor, and the Heir of all things.*
The time is coming, when death shall be destroyed; this is the
last enemy. Christ shall reign till He has put all enemies
under His feet. But were it possible for the animals to be
retained by the power of Satan in death, there then would still
be an enemy for Christ to subdue; but as Christ shall most
certainly triumph over all His enemies, and as death is one,
then He shall restore life unto all which once enjoyed it."

And thus Dr. Adam Clarke :—

" I. The brute creation never sinned against God, nor are
they capable of it; and, consequently, cannot be liable to
punishment.

" II. But the whole brute creation is in a suffering state, and
partake of the common infirmities and privations, as well as
mankind; they suffer, but who can say they suffer justly ?

" III. As they appear to be necessarily involved in the sufferings of sinful man, and yet neither through their fault nor

folly, it is natural to suppose that the Judge of all the earth, who ever does right, will find some means by which these innocent creatures shall be compensated for their sufferings.

" IV. That they have no compensation here, their afflictions, labours, and death, prove; and if they are to have any compensation, they must have it in another state.

" V. God, the Fountain of all goodness, must have originally designed them for that measure of happiness which is suited to the powers with which he had endowed them; but since the fall of man they never had that happiness, and in their present circumstances never can.

" VI. As to intelligent beings, God has formed his purposes in reference to their happiness, on the ground of their rational natures. He has decreed that they shall be happy if they will, all the means of it being placed within their power; and if they be ultimately miserable, it is the effect of their own unconstrained choice; therefore His purpose is fulfilled, either in their happiness or misery, because He has purposed that they shall be happy if they please, and that misery shall be the result of their refusal.

" VII. But it does not appear that the brute creation are capable of this choice, and it is evident that they are not placed in their present misery through either their choice or sin; and if no purpose of God can be ultimately frustrated, these creatures must be restored to that state of happiness for which they have been made, and of which they have been deprived through the transgression of man.

" VIII. To say that the enjoyments which they have in this life are a sufficient compensation, is most evidently false; for had sin not entered into the world, they would have had much greater enjoyments, without pain, excessive labour, and toil, and without death, and all their sufferings which arise from its pre-disposing causes. Nor does it appear that they have much happiness from eating, drinking, and the rest, as they have these only in the proportion in which they are necessary to their existence, as the slaves of men. Therefore, allowing that they have even enjoyment and gratification in life, they have much less than they would have had, had not sin entered into the world; and, consequently, they have been deprived of the greater portion of happiness designed for them by their bountiful Creator.

" IX. It is therefore obvious, that the gracious purpose of God has not been fulfilled in them; and that as they have not lost their happiness through their own fault, both the beneficence and justice of God are bound to make them reparation.

" X. Hence it is reasonable to conclude, that as from the present constitution of things, they cannot have the happiness designed for them in this state, they must have it in another."

And so once more, the Rev. Daniel Isaac :—" The rational creation was made subject to vanity or trouble willingly; for the sin of our first parents was certainly wilful. If it be objected that their posterity are subjected to trouble not willingly, I answer, that the Apostle by the word ' was ' evidently refers to the period when vanity was first introduced into the creation ; and it can be true of the irrational creation only, that at that time it 'was made subject to vanity not willingly.'" . . . . " The Apostle observes, that ' the whole creation groaneth and travaileth in pain together until now.' And what are they groaning and travailing for ? ' To be delivered from the bondage of corruption, into the glorious liberty of the children of God.' This is true of the irrational creation. But no one pretends that the whole of men and devils had groaned and travailed until the Apostle's time to enjoy 'the glorious liberty of the children of God.' . . . . Rational creatures in this passage are distinguished from the creation, for the earnest expectation of the *creature* (Της Κτισεως *creation)* waiteth for the manifestation of the *Sons of God.* Because the *creature (creation)* itself shall be delivered from the bondage of corruption into the. glorious liberty of *the children of God.* For we know that the *whole creation* groaneth and travaileth in pain together until now ; and *not only they* but *ourselves* also, which have the first fruits of the Spirit, &c."

The following is an extract from a work by the Rev. John Hildrop, D.D.—" Do you think it a breach of natural justice, without necessity, to take away the life of any creature? And can you think that Infinite Mercy who made them to be happy, could, in the primary intention of their nature, resolve to deprive them of that happiness, or at least, a possibility of recovering it again, by an utter extinction of their being? But some serious writers on this subject tell us their existence was given them on this very condition, that it should be temporary and short; that after they had fluttered, or crept, or swam, or walked about their respective elements, for a little season, they should be swept away by the hands of violence, or the course of nature, into an entire extinction of being, to make room for their successors in the same circle of vanity and corruption. But pray, Who told them so? Does reason or Revelation countenance in the least such a bold assertion? So far from it, that it seems in direct contradiction to both. The wise preacher has given as a a deeper foundation for our philosophy,—ECCLESIASTES iii. 14. 'I know that whatsoever GOD doeth, it shall be for ever; nothing can be put to it, nor any thing taken from it: and GOD doeth it that men should fear before Him." Again, "Who can fix the direct point where the last dying sound expires in dead silence? Who can discern where the last glimmering ray of light is smothered up in total darkness? Who can determine the limits betwixt the ebbing and flowing of the tide, or describe the single point which is the ending of the one, and beginning of the other? Nor are the boundaries betwixt the human and brute understanding more easily distinguished. Who can determine the lowest degree of human ignorance, and the highest pitch of animal knowledge? Who can say where the one ends and the other begins, or whether there be any other difference betwixt them, but only in degree?'" . . . . "Shall the eternal purposes of infinite wisdom, love, and power, be entirely defeated by the malice of evil spirits, and the infirmities of frail creatures? To say that the animals shall be annihilated, is in effect to say, that the Almighty Creator, the Father of mercies, and the God of all compassion, whose mercies are over all His works, is either unwilling or unable to effect the eternal purposes of His infinite love! that the devil is more powerful to destroy than God to save!"

Thus, also, Matthew Henry, in his *Commentary*, (on Romans viii. 19—22.) "There shall be a glory conferred upon all the creatures, which shall be (in the proportion of their natures) as suitable and as great an advancement as the glory of the children of God shall be to them. The fire at the last day shall be a refining—not a destroying annihilating fire. What becomes of the souls of the brutes, that go downwards, none

2 B

can tell. But it should seem by the Scripture, that there will
be some kind of restoration of them. And if it be objected,
what use will they be of to glorified saints? we may suppose
them of as much use as they were to Adam in innocency; and
if it be only to illustrate the wisdom, power, and goodness of
their Creator, that is enough."

So, too, Dr. Hitchcock, in his *Religion of Geology*, says,—
"Whether the inferior animals will exist again after death, is a
more doubtful point. There is certainly nothing in Scripture
against their future existence; for the passage in the Psalms,
which says, that 'man that is in honour and abideth not, is like
the brutes that perish,' if understood to mean the annihilation
of animals, would prove also the annihilation of wicked men.
And while most men of learning and piety have suspended
their opinion on the existence of the inferior animals after
death, for want of evidence, some have been decided advocates
of the future happy existence of all beings who exhibit a spark
of intelligence. Not a few distinguished German theologians
and philosophers regard the whole visible creation, both animate and inanimate, as at present in a confined and depressed
state, and struggling for freedom. On this principle, Tholuck
explains that most difficult passage in Romans, which declares
that ' the whole creation groaneth and travaileth in pain
together until now.' He supposes this 'bound or fettered state
of nature,' both animate and inanimate, to have a casual con-
nection with sin, and the death accompanying it among men;
and, therefore, when men are freed from sin and death, 'the
creature itself also shall be delivered from the bondage of
corruption into the glorious liberty of the children of God.'
The kingdom of God, according to Tholuck, Martin Luther,

17

and many other distinguished theologians, will not be transferred to heaven at the end of the world, but be established on
earth, where all these transformations of the animate and
inanimate creation will take place. This exposition surely
carries with it a great deal of naturalness and probability ; and
if it be true, death to the inferior animals must surely be an
indication of great benevolence on the part of the Deity, since
it introduces them to a higher state of existence."

And, lastly, Mr. J. T. Gray, in a pamphlet on *Immortality :*
—" In the insect transformation, we see clearly, that under an
apparent disorganization of frame, the germ of existence may
be yet preserved; that an entire suspension of animation is not
identical with its extinction; and that a change, which to the
eye may be unpleasing, may yet be the natural process of
transition to a higher state of being."

Next, then, as to the reasons which may be supposed to have
seemed sufficient to those great and eminent men first named,
and the others I have quoted from, as a foundation for their
deliberate opinions thus expressed, regarding the future existence of animals. First, there are those derivable from Scripture,
and, secondly, those suggested by observation and reflection on
the proofs which the actions of animals have, in all ages and
countries, afforded of their mental capacities. These will
speak for themselves. It will be sufficient to say for the
present, that it seems impossible to attach the idea of extinction or annihilation to anything that is not material. We
argue the truth of man's immortality from the fact that he is
capable of losing any part or many parts of his body, without
his soul or any of the faculties of his mind being destroyed or
one whit injured or affected. Why not give animals the

benefit of a like argument? They, like ourselves, have mental capacities, similarly provable to be distinct from and independant of their bodies, and, as will be abundantly seen in the course of the following pages, in many respects not inferior, and in some superior, to our own. The destruction of a body, its dissolution into its component elements, we can conceive, and we can see; but a spirit has no parts, and into what then can a spirit, whether of animal or man, be dissolved?

As to the testimony of Scripture:—"Although it is not the scope of revelation to satisfy curiosity on a multitude of interesting enquiries that suggest themselves to the thoughtful reader, nevertheless it is permissible to collect any scattered rays which may partially enlighten us, even on subjects apart from the grand and immediate objects for which Scripture was given."*

Unfounded as the idea of immortality being the heritage of the animal creation may at first appear to some, yet it will be seen that there are no express passages of Holy Scripture to contradict, while there are some that appear to sanction it; so that although such a doctrine is not to be dogmatically laid down as an article of belief, there is yet enough to vindicate it from a charge of mere speculativeness.       .

Adam by his sin brought death into the world. When he was created, he found all creatures living, and all pronounced " very good;" and it seems unreasonable to suppose that any beings were intended for annihilation, on which such a benediction was pronounced by their Creator. The first and main object of their being called into existence, was His glory, and

* Scriptural Probabilities as to a Resurrection of the Brute Creation, London, J. H. Campbell. A Pamphlet to which I am much indebted in these remarks.

secondly, the benefit of man. Even as it is, since the Fall, it is but a very small proportion of animated nature that directly subserves his use. If it be objected that they serve to manifest the wisdom of God in creation, His power, and His goodness, it is to be replied that so, and much more, they will, if resuscitated for an eternal existence beyond the period of their present short-lived and transitory one. Besides which, the vast and incalculable majority of the various creatures live and die utterly out of and beyond the reach or observation of man, so that they cannot be the medium or cause of any praise ascending on their account, through cognizance of them, from him to GOD.

It was the same SPIRIT of GOD that "breathed into man's nostrils the breath of life," that gave the same animal life to creatures. Thus says Isaiah, xxxii. 15, "Thou sendest forth Thy SPIRIT, they are created."

It is therefore of GOD that there is something solemn in the death of every living creature. No one can watch without any emotion the eye glazing in death of a faithful dog or horse, the mild look of a dying bird, or the expiring throb of a wounded animal. Who can avoid the thought that something is going away which he cannot bring back, nor any power of his then stay, even for awhile, the departure of ? And if it be some long known and favourite companion, conspicuous perhaps for fidelity, affection, and sagacity, whose bodily life is ebbing away,—who is there who can resist the thought, that he is not parting with the dying creature for ever, but that the same CREATOR who gave the spirit, and now commands it to "return," will one day restore it, and bid it live again? It is repulsive to our natural feeling to think that anything in the nature of spiritual life can be annihilated. The idea of the death of a body, and of its being doomed to destruction, is of itself sad and painful : the thought of the simultaneous destruction of the spirit, our own soul resists. We are forced by a natural impulse to ask whether the living spirit in any creature, is not too much the breath of God, to cease to live, and perish with the body ? whether it may not have been intended by the Almighty to live hereafter, and for ever, restored to a renewed body, even as we ourselves look to be to our own ? whether it is not of too noble and excellent a nature to perish for ever, and "may not, in the case of the irrational but irresponsible and innocent part of the animated creation, be restored in a better and an everlasting state?" The ways indeed of God, "are not as our ways, nor His thoughts as our thoughts," but on no other supposition can we at present see any compensation, as there then abundantly would be,—(not that He, the Sovereign Creator "of His own will" of all, is bound to make compensation)—for the sufferings and death of the creatures, the necessary consequence of the fall of man, and too frequently aggravated unnecessarily by him.

From the very beginning of the Bible onwards to its close, we find the animal creation associated with man, both in the blessing and the curse. They were both alike pronounced "very good" in the primæval world. They were both made sufferers by the Fall,—were both overwhelmed by the destruction of the Flood,—were both preserved in the Ark,—both shared in the greatest and last plague of Egypt,—both in the hallowing of the first-born—both in the rest of the Sabbath. Animals were made to suffer with men in the punishment of a city that should fall into idolatry. They suffered with Achan in the judgment upon him, with the men of Benjamin, in the destruction inflicted upon them, and with the men of Jerusalem when subdued by the Chaldeans. They were included in the doom pronounced on Babylon, on Edom, and on Egypt. They were not forgotten in the mercy showed to Nineveh on its repentance, and were to be made partakers in the plague pronounced on the enemies of Jerusalem. " In these and other instances, we perceive how uniformly the lower sentient creation has partaken of the destiny of man, whether in general, or in particular cases; how it has been included in the Lord's past grand dispensational arrangements for the world, from Adam to the times of the Gentiles, commencing with Nebuchadnezzar, and still continuing. And the prophetic page clearly intimates its participation in the blessing of the reign of CHRIST. For the idea that, after all this, it will not have a place in the ultimate perfection of all things, no valid reason can be adduced."*

It is evident that animals were in a very different state in Paradise from that into which they came through the Fall. The fear and dread of man were not at first upon them: these came with the curse ; but afterwards the creatures were taken with Noah and his seed into an everlasting covenant with GOD, a fact repeated no less than five times to impress its importance on us. In the Millennium all things will be subdued to CHRIST, "all sheep and oxen, yea and the beasts of the field, the fowl of the air, and the fishes of the sea, and whatsoever passeth through the paths of the sea." Then the "leopard shall lie down with the kid, and the lion shall eat straw like the ox ; they shall not hurt nor destroy in all my holy mountain, saith

* The New Heavens and the New Earth, by George G. Walker, London, Kent and Co.

the Lord." And does it seem reasonable to think, that after
this restoration with man to somewhat of their primæval state
in Paradise, all living creatures should, at the conclusion of that
epoch, instead of sharing with man in his next and highest
elevation, be devoted to a sudden and eternal extinction?
that having once fallen with man they should not rise with him?
Can we suppose that these creatures of GOD's hand are to have
no share in the " Restitution of all things," "the reconciling of
all things to Himself," " whether things in earth or things in
Heaven," in the " times of refreshing from the presence of the
LORD," " according to the good pleasure which He hath purposed in Himself, that in the dispensation of the fulness of time
He might gather together in one all things in CHRIST, both
which are in Heaven, and which are on earth."

If we were to think so, we must conclude that animals will
be in an inferior condition at the close of the Millennium to what
they will have been placed in at its commencement, and that
Paradise Restored will have no place for the creatures who had
a position in the first Paradise which they lost, through no sin
of their own, but only through that of man.

" But no passage hitherto produced" I quote from the work
already referred to, "seems to countenance the doctrine of a
resurrection of the brute creation, so much as Rom. viii.
19—22, 'For the earnest expectation of the creation waiteth
for the manifestation of the sons of God. For the creation
was made subject to vanity, (not willingly, but by reason
of him who hath subjected [it]) in hope; because the
creation itself also shall be delivered from the bondage of
corruption into the liberty of the glory of the children of God.
For we know that the whole creation groaneth and travaileth

in pain together until now. And not only [it], &c. That
κτίσις means here the created universe is admitted by many,
and this is its ordinary sense in the New Testament. Indeed
some are of opinion that it is never there used of *mankind alone.*
From verse 23, it is seen to be distinct from Christians, and it
cannot be understood of those who are not Christians, who in
no sense could be said to wait for the manifestation of the sons
of God. Understanding it then of creation in its simplest,
broadest meaning, we learn that this was involuntarily subjected
to vanity by God; (in consequence, as we know, of man's fall;)
but that it is not hopelessly ruined, but awaits, while every
where expressing the language of pain and suffering, a period
of emancipation from its bondage. That this period will be
fully reached during the Millennium it is impossible to conceive,
for reasons already stated. But in the then *manifested* and
glorified sons of God an earnest will be afforded to the
creation, already greatly advanced in the scale of happiness,
of what its ultimate and *perfect* state is destined to be. And
again may the former argument be pressed. If animals, which
not the least of the creation, share the common travail, and
not least express their sense of it,—if animals will partake of
the blessings connected with the revelation of the sons of God,
and in their measure keep pace with the improved circumstances
of 'regeneration,' what valid objection can be raised to their
participation in 'the liberty of the glory' of the redeemed?
And would not that imply their resurrection? And if recovery,
not annihilation, is God's purpose for the creation as a whole,
why should not animal life, so conspicuous and wonderful a
portion of that creation, be restored rather than annihilated?
So far as we can judge at present, this idea best suits the

passage before us.   It is difficult, with the bright and gladden-
ing prospect it unfolds, to come to the conclusion that living
creatures, far below man indeed in dignity, yet still raised
above mere inanimate objects by their peculiar characteristics,
—creatures that owe their manifold living and dying pains to a
cause to which they in no wise contributed,—shall finally not
only be excluded from the universal jubilee of creation, but
cease to belong to it at all.   Would not this rather look like
a triumph of the bondage of corruption than a deliverance from
it?   Would it not be like being borne along the stream of
progressive bliss, only to be finally engulphed in the abyss
of oblivion?   And does it appear altogether in unison with
the splendid anticipations inspired by this Scripture, that
the groans of the sentient, though irrational, part of the
creation, should ultimately, alone of all the other, not be
changed to the notes of joy, but cease (and that, too, after
a bright gleam of hope) in the silence of endless death? "

" We will now see if there be any passages of Scripture which
clearly negative the idea of dead animals also having an interest
in a future life.   A person who should search for such, would,
probably, be surprised how few can be adduced which even
have the appearance of being opposed to such an idea.   The only
two that will, probably, be found, are Psalm xlix. 12, 20, and
Ecclesiastes iii. 21.   As to the first, it is at least an open question
whether we should render ' He is like the beasts *(that) perish;* '
or, ' He is like the beasts, *they are alike.*'   But even retaining
the common version, the meaning will be, man abideth not in
honour, but death takes him off in the midst of his pride and
complacency, not less than it does the mere beasts; which he,
indeed, having no understanding, resembles.   Thus nothing is

got from this place, that is at all adverse to beasts enjoying a
future life. For it will not be said, that worldly men resemble
beasts, in that both the one and the other absolutely perish, in
the sense of ceasing to exist for ever.

"In Ecclesiastes iii. 18—21, Solomon views man's life from the
standing point of purely natural perception. To an observer
'under the sun,' there was no perceptible difference between
the life and death of a man and of a beast; the pre-eminence
of the former being determined alone by *revelation*: and so he
adds parenthetically, 'Who knoweth the spirit of man, that
goeth upward, and the spirit of the beast that goeth downward to the earth?' As much as to say, the superiority
of man's spirit is solely established by what God has
taught, not by human observation. What this superiority is,
is but obscurely made known in *this* place. Comparing it with
chap. xii. 7, we may infer that the human spirit, after the
dissolution of the body, is especially perserved by God; probably
signified by its 'going upward,' while an inferior destiny awaits
the spirit of the beast, that is said to 'go downward to the
earth.' That this phrase, however, is equivalent to utter
destruction, may be questioned, both because that idea is not
necessarily conveyed by the words, and because it is easily
conceivable that the destiny of the spirit of man is the higher,
without considering that it is so only by contrast with the
annihilation of the other. And even if we suppose every
faculty of sensation to be suspended or extinguished at its
death, a return to life could not be pronounced impossible.
Even in this case it might be said, why should it be thought a
thing incredible that God should raise the dead? Omnipotence
could raise the bodies that have been dissolved, and again 'cause

breath to enter' into them. The Psalmist, speaking of man, says, 'His breath goeth forth, he returneth to his earth; in that very day his thoughts perish.' (Ps. cxlvi. 4.) Supposing we had only passages like this, and others similar, (as Ps. xlix. 19; Job xiv. 10—12,) what ideas should we have been likely to entertain of *our own* destiny? And when, in words so very similar, we read of the brute creation, 'Thou hidest thy face, they are troubled; thou takest away their breath, they die, and return to their dust,' (Ps. civ. 29,) is it not very conceivable that, had equally full light been given us about *their* future, as we possess about our own, the hasty verdict that excludes them from immortality would have no countenance? The fact is, seeing that life and death are both mysteries to us, and (apart from what Scripture says) only known by their effects, a little less positiveness than is common in determining things connected with them were more suitable."

Secondly, as to the proofs of the mental capacities of animals furnished by their actions. The anecdotes themselves which I have collected together, will, in my opinion, furnish abundant evidence of their powers, and I shall leave them, as I have already said, to speak for themselves, believing with Locke, that they make it "as evident that some animals do in certain instances reason, as that they have sense." "Knowest thou not," says Milton, "their knowledge and their ways? They also know and reason not contemptibly." Thus Aristotle, also, "There are between man and animals faculties in common, near and analagous," "In taking a review," says Schleiden, of most, if not all of the actions of the animal world, it must be obvious that, whether we allow them reason or not, the actions themselves comprehend these elements of reason, so to speak, which we commonly refer to rational beings. So that if the same actions had been done by our fellow-creatures, we should have ascribed them without hesitation to motives and feelings worthy of a rational nature. It is certain that most animals, in their several rational acts, show every outward sign of consciousness, or knowledge of the end of their actions, not like the fixed and uninformed operations of instinct, which is wholly employed in their self preservation, or in providing for their young. If we compare our own mental constitution with that of brutes, however we may excel them, as we certainly do in some noble capacities and principles exclusively belonging to our moral nature, yet we possess many faculties and powers precisely analogous to theirs; and the motives and combined operations of these, it is often as difficult to understand as it is those of the lower animals."

From all that has been advanced, I think it must be confessed by every candid person, that there is much in favour of the notion that the spiritual life of animals is not extinguished at the time of their bodily death, and that the most that can be said in opposition to the idea, is only, in the words of Sir Edward Lytton Bulwer, that they have " no warrant of an hereafter :" I dare not, and do not, affirm that they have; but I do say, " Why should it be thought a thing incredible that God should raise the dead," in the case of the animal creation, any more than in that of men?—God, " in whose hand is the soul of every living thing, and the breath of all mankind."

c

The Authorities for the Anecdotes will be found in the Index at the end of the Volume.

# RECORDS

OF

# ANIMAL SAGACITY AND CHARACTER.

——o•o¦•¦o•o——

THERE is no way in which the young can better learn the sentiments of devotion, or the old preserve them, than by cultivating those habits of thought and observation, which convert the scenes of Nature into the temple of God; which make us see the Deity in every appearance we behold, and change the world, in which the ignorant and the thoughtless see only the reign of time and chance, into the kingdom of the living and ever present God of the Universe.—ALISON.

# THE DOG.

1. The wisest dog I ever had, said Sir Walter Scott, was what is called the bull-dog terrier. I taught him to understand a great many words, insomuch that I am positive that the communication betwixt the canine species and ourselves might be greatly enlarged. Camp once bit the baker, who was bringing bread to the family,—I beat him, and explained the enormity of his offence; after which, to the last moment of his life, he never heard the least allusion to the story, in whatever voice or tone it was mentioned, without getting up and retiring into the darkest corner of the room, with great appearance of distress. Then if you said, the baker was well paid, or, the baker was not hurt after all, Camp came forth from his hiding-place, capered, and barked, and rejoiced. When he was unable, towards the end of his life, to attend me when on horseback, he used to watch for my return, and the servant would tell him his master was coming down the hill, or through the moor, and although he did not use any gesture to explain his meaning, Camp was never known to mistake him, but either went out at the front to go up the hill, or at the back to get down to the moor-side. He certainly had a singular knowledge of spoken language

2. Sir Walter Scott has also told a number of anecdotes of a dog called Dandie, the property of a another

2 c

gentleman, which knew on most occasions what was said
in his presence. His master returning home one night
rather late, found all the family in bed, and not being
able to find the boot-jack in its usual place, said to his
dog, " Dandie, I cannot find my boot-jack ; search for
it." The dog, quite sensible of what had been said to
him, scratched at the room door which his master
opened, proceeded to a distant part of the house, and
soon returned, carrying in his mouth the boot-jack,
which his master had left that morning under a sofa.

3. That they in reality learn, say the Messrs.
Chambers of Edinburgh, in their Anecdotes of Dogs, to
know the meaning of certain words, not merely when
addressed to them, but when spoken in ordinary conversation, is beyond a doubt, although the accompanying looks and movements in all likelihood help them in
their interpretation. We have known a small spaniel,
for instance, which thoroughly understood the meaning
of " out," or " going out," when spoken in the most
casual way in conversation.

4. They add—a lady of our acquaintance has a dog
which lives at enmity with another dog in the neighbour
hood, called York, and angrily barks when the word
York is pronounced in his hearing.

5. The late Dr. J. Maculloch has related, of his own
knowledge, that a shepherd's dog always eluded the
intentions of the household regarding him, if aught was
whispered in his presence that did not coincide with his
wishes.

6. James Hogg, in his Shepherd's Calendar, declares
that dogs know what is said on subjects in which they

feel interested. A farmer, had a dog that for the space of three or four years, in the latter part of his life, met him always at the foot of his farm, about a mile and a half from his house, on his way home. If he was half a day away, a week, or a fortnight, it was all the same; she met him at that spot; and there never was an instance seen of her going to wait his arrival there on a wrong day. She could only know of his coming home by hearing it mentioned in the family.

7. The same writer speaks of a clever sheep-dog, named Hector, which had a similar tact in picking up what was said. One day he observed to his mother, " I am going to-morrow to Bowerhope for a fortnight; but I will not take Hector with me, for he is constantly quarrelling with the rest of the dogs." Hector, who was present, and overheard the conversation, was missing next morning, and when Hogg reached Bower-hope, there was Hector sitting on a knoll, waiting his arrival. He had swam across a flooded river to reach the spot.

8. Still more surprising, say the Messrs. Chambers, dogs may be trained not only to know the meaning of words, but to speak them. The learned Leibnitz reported to the French Academy, that he had seen a dog in Germany which had been taught to pronounce certain words. The teacher of the animal, he stated, was a Saxon peasant boy, who, having observed in the dog's voice an indistinct resemblance to various sounds of the human voice, was prompted to endeavour to make him speak. The animal was three years old at the beginning of his instructions, a circumstance which

must have been unfavourable to the object; yet, by dint
of great labour and perseverance, in three years the boy
had taught it to pronounce thirty German words.  It
used to astonish its visitors by calling for tea, coffee,
chocolate, &c.: but it is proper to remark, that it
required its master to pronounce the words beforehand;
and it never appeared to become quite reconciled to the
exhibitions it was forced to make.

9. Reason, says our great lexicographer, is the
power by which we deduce one proposition from
another, or proceed from premises to consequences.
I wanted one day to go through a tall iron gate, from
one part of my premises to another, but just within it
lay a poor lame puppy, and I could not get in without
rolling the little fellow over, and perhaps seriously
injuring him.  I stood for a while hesitating, and at
length determined to go round, through another gate,
when a fine Newfoundland dog, who had been waiting
patiently for his wonted caresses, and wondering why
I did not come in, looked accidentally down at the
invalid.  He comprehended the whole business in a
moment.  He put down his great paw, and as quickly
and as gently as possible rolled the invalid out of the
way, and then drew himself back in order to leave room
for the opening of the gate.  Here was a plain and
palpable act of reasoning.  " Why does not my master
come in as usual?  This little fellow is in the way, and
he cannot open the gate without disturbing or hurting
him.  I'll get rid of that;" and immediately he rolls
the obstacle aside, but, with the characteristic noble
feeling of his breed, he takes care not to hurt the

invalid. "Now," he continues, "I must take myself out of the way, and then every obstacle will be removed." No philosopher ever reasoned more accurately than our beautiful Newfoundland dog. No one ever drew more legitimate consequences from certain existing premises.

10. There is a nobleness of feeling of a similar nature in the Newfoundland dog, and in most of the larger species of dogs. Dr. Abell, in one of his lectures on phrenology, related a very striking anecdote of a Newfoundland dog in Cork. This dog was of a noble and generous disposition, and when he left his master's house, was often assailed by several little noisy curs in the street. He usually passed them with apparent unconcern, as if they were beneath his notice; but one little brute was particularly troublesome, and at length, carried his petulance so far as to bite the Newfoundland dog in the back of his leg. This was a degree of wanton insult which could not be patiently endured, and he instantly turned round, ran after the offender, and seized him by the poll. In this manner he carried him to the quay, and holding him for some time over the water, at length dropped him into it. He did not, however, design that the culprit should be capitally punished; he waited a little while, until the offender was not only well ducked, but near sinking, and then he plunged in and brought him out safe to land. It would be difficult, says the doctor, to conceive of any punishment more aptly contrived, or more completely in character. A variety of comparisons, and motives, and generous feelings, entered into the composition of this act.

11. This seems almost ᵗ ιcredible, but I remember reading an anecdote, which, ᵗs far as I can remember, was authenticated when published. A gentleman used to go twice a year to London, and remain near a week, leaving his horse at St. Albans, and going to and from thence by coach. He chanced, one journey, to have a small dog with him, and that he left with the horse at St. Albans. Returning at the end of a week, he was told, by the hostler, that on the day he (the gentleman) started for London, the innkeeper's dog broke loose and fixed on the other; when separated, the stranger bolted, and next day returning with a large Newfoundland dog, the two deliberately walked up to the offender, and after giving him a terrible punishment, departed, and had not been seen since. The Newfoundland dog being then described—oh ! said the gentleman, it's all right: the small dog had been home (twenty miles) and fetched his companion to help him in his revenge on mine host's Cerberus.

12. A gentleman residing in Fifeshire, and not far from the city of St. Andrews, was in possession of a very fine Newfoundland dog, which was remarkable alike for its tractability and its trust-worthiness. At two other points, each distant about a mile, and at the same distance from this gentleman's mansion, there were two dogs of great power, but of less tractable breeds than the Newfoundland one. One of these was a large mastiff, kept as a watch-dog by a farmer, and the other a staunch bull-dog, that kept guard over the parish mill. As each of these three was lord-ascendant of all animals at his master's residence, they all had a

good deal of aristocratic pride and pugnacity, so that
two of them seldom met without attempting to settle
their respective dignities by a wager of battle. The
Newfoundland dog was of some service in the domestic
arrangements, besides his guardianship of the house ;
for every forenoon he was sent to the baker's shop in
the village, about half a mile distant, with a towel
containing money in the corner, and he returned with
the value of the money in bread. There were many
useless and not over civil curs in the village, as there
are in too many villages throughout the country ; but
ordinarily the haughty Newfoundland treated this
ignoble race in that contemptuous style in which great
dogs are wont to treat little ones. When the dog
returned from the baker's shop, he used to be regularly
served with his dinner, and went peaceably on house
duty for the rest of the day. One day, however, he
returned with his coat dirtied and his ears scratched,
having been subjected to a combined attack of the
curs while he had charge of his towel and bread, and
so could not defend himself. Instead of waiting for
his dinner as usual, he laid down his charge somewhat
sulkily, and marched off; and upon looking after him,
it was observed that he was crossing the intervening
hollow in a straight line for the house of the farmer,
or rather on an embassy to the farmer's mastiff. The
farmer's people noticed this unusual visit, and they
were induced to notice it from its being a meeting of
peace between those who had habitually been belliger-
ents. After some intercourse, of which no interpretation could be given, the two set off together in the

direction of the mill; and having arrived there, they
in brief space engaged the miller's bull-dog as an ally.
The straight road to the village where the indignity
had been offered to the Newfoundland dog passed
immediately in front of his master's house, but there
was a more private and more circuitous road by the
back of the mill. The three took this road, reached
the village, scoured it in great wrath, putting to the
tooth every cur they could get sight of, and, having
taken their revenge, and washed themselves in a ditch,
they returned, each dog to the abode of his master;
and when any two of them happened to meet afterwards, they displayed the same pugnacity as they had
done previous to this joint expedition.

13. There is another well authenticated anecdote of
two dogs at Donaghadee, in which the instinctive daring
of the one in behalf of the other caused a friendship,
and, as it should seem, a kind of lamentation for the
dead, after one of them had paid the debt of nature.
This happened while the government harbour or pier
for the packets at Donaghadee was in the course of
building, and it took place in the sight of several
witnesses. The one dog, in this case also, was a Newfoundland, and the other was a mastiff. They were
both powerful dogs, and though each was good natured
when alone, they were very much in the habit of
fighting when they met. One day they had a fierce
and prolonged battle on the pier, from the point of
which they both fell into the sea; and as the pier was
long and steep, they had no means of escape but by
swimming a considerable distance. Throwing water

upon fighting dogs is an approved means of putting
an end to their hostilities; and, it is natural to suppose,
that two combatants of the same species tumbling
themselves into the sea would have the same effect.
It had, and each began to make for the land as he
best could. The Newfoundland being an excellent
swimmer, very speedily gained the pier, on which he
stood shaking himself, but at the same time watching
the motions of his late antagonist, who being no
swimmer, was struggling exhausted in the water, and
just about to sink. In dashed the Newfoundland dog,
took the other gently by the collar, kept his head above
water, and brought him safely on shore. There was a
peculiar kind of recognition between the two animals
—they never fought again—they were always together
—and when the Newfoundland dog had been accidentally killed by the passage of a stone wagon on the
railway over him, the other languished and evidently
lamented for a long time.

14. I am so satisfied that dogs, and many, if not all,
other animals have language or other means of impart-
ing their thoughts, that I am almost afraid of beginning
recital of proof; but, to insure the reader against tiring
his patience,—only one instance of the faculty. My friend
Doctor F. H. M. has told me of his father's dog, Jem,
who was not renowned as a fighting dog, and having
sometimes to pay a visit to some canine friend in the
locality, he would have to pass the parsonage house,
where was a dog a little too much for Jem, but afraid
of Jem's companion, Carlo, who, therefore, on being
politely requested by Jem, used to escort him past the

other, and then return home. Jem was a dog well
known for miles round,—a dog that would not be picked
up by any one, and that fact renders the following still
more wonderful. Doctor M's father was on his death-
bed; Jem, who was ardently attached to his master,
could not be kept from the chamber. Immediately Mr.
M. breathed his last, the groom was started on horseback to inform the sister. The groom, as was his
custom, whistled and called for Jem, but to no purpose;
—returned from his journey of seven or eight miles, he
was asked if the dog did not go with him. No! he had
not seen him. The crier was employed, the dog was
advertized, and was well known, but never was seen or
heard of from the moment the soul of his master had
left its earthly tenement. Will any one say that the
faithful creature did not go to some secluded spot and
die of grief?

15 We read of a surgeon who found a poor dog with
his leg broken. He took him home, set the leg, and
in due time gave the dog his liberty. Some months
afterwards, the surgeon was awoke in the night by a
dog barking loudly at his door. As the barking continued, and the surgeon thought he recognized the
voice, he got up and went down stairs. When he
opened the door, there stood his former patient
wagging his tail, and by his side another dog—a friend
whom he had brought—who had also had the misfortune to get a leg broken.

16 The following anecdotes illustrate in a remarkable manner the devoted attachment of dogs to their
masters:—An officer named St. Leger, who was im-

prisoned in Vincennes, near Paris, during the wars of
St. Bartholomew, wished to keep with him a greyhound
that he had brought up, and which was much attached
to him; but they harshly refused him this innocent
pleasure, and sent away the greyhound to his house in
the Rue des Lions Saint Paul. The next day, the
greyhound returned alone to Vincennes, and began to
bark under the windows of the tower, towards the
place where the officer was confined. St. Leger
approached, looked through the bars, and was delighted
again to see his faithful hound, who began to jump and
play a thousand gambols to show her joy. Her master
threw a piece of bread to the animal, who ate it with
great good will. St. Leger did the same in his prison,
and in spite of the immense wall which separated
them, they breakfasted together like two friends. This
friendly visit was not the last. Abandoned by his
relations, who believed him dead, the unfortunate
prisoner received the visits of his greyhound only,
during four years confinement. Whatever weather it
might be, in spite of rain or snow, the faithful animal
did not fail a single day to pay her accustomed visit.
Six months after his release from prison, St. Leger
died. The faithful greyhound would no longer remain
in the house, but, on the day after the funeral, returned
to the castle of Vincennes, and it is supposed she was
actuated by a motive of gratitude. A jailer of the
outer court, had always shown great kindness to this
dog, which was as handsome as affectionate, Contrary
to the custom of people of that class, this man had
been touched by her attachment and beauty, so that he

facilitated her approach to see her master, and also insured her a safe retreat. Penetrated with gratitude for this service, the greyhound remained the rest of her life near the benevolent jailer. It was remarked, that even while testifying her zeal and gratitude for her second master, one could easily see that her heart was with the first. Like those, who, having lost a parent, a brother, or a friend, come from afar to seek consolation by viewing the place which they inhabited, this affectionate animal repaired frequently to the tower where St. Leger had been imprisoned, and would contemplate for hours together the gloomy window from which her master had so often smiled to her, and where they had so frequently breakfasted together.

17. In January, 1799, the cold was so intense that the Seine was frozen to the depth of fifteen or sixteen inches. Following the example of a number of thoughtless youths who were determined to continue the amusement of skating, in spite of a thaw having commenced, a young student, called Beaumanoir, wished also to partake of this dangerous pleasure, near the quay of the Hotel des Monnaies, of Paris; but he had scarcely gone twenty steps when the ice broke under his weight, and he disappeared. The young skater had carried a small spaniel with him, which, seeing his master sink under the ice, immediately gave the alarm by barking with all his might, near the spot where the accident had happened. It will easily be believed that it was impossible to give any assistance to the unfortunate youth, but the howlings of the animal warned others from approaching the fatal place. The

poor spaniel sent forth the most frightful howls; he
ran along the river as if he were mad; and at last, not
seeing his master return, he went to establish himself
at the hole where he had seen him disappear, and
there he passed the rest of the day and all the following night. The day after, people saw with surprise
the poor animal sorrowfully at the same post. Struck
with admiration of such constancy, some of them made
him a little bed of straw, and brought him some food;
but, absorbed in the most profound grief, he would not
even drink the milk which these kind-hearted people
placed near him. Sometimes he would run about the
ice or the borders of the river to seek his master, but
he always returned to sleep in the same place. He bit
a soldier who was attempting to make him leave his
inhospitable retreat, who, fearing that he was mad,
fired at and wounded him. This affecting example of
grief and constancy was witnessed for many days, and
people came in crowds to contemplate this beautiful
trait of attachment, which was not without its reward.
The dog being only slightly wounded, was taken charge
of by a woman, who, compassionating his suffering,
and touched by the affection he showed for his late
master, carried him to her house, where his wound was
dressed, and every effort that kindness could devise
was practised, to console him for the loss of the young
skater.

18. A short time ago, a dog, well known to the
railway officials from his frequent travelling with his
master, presented himself at one of the stations on the
Fleetwood, Preston, and Longridge line. After looking

D

round for some length of time amongst the passengers
and in the carriages, just as the train was about to
start he leaped into one of the compartments of a
carriage, and laid himself down under the seat.
Arriving at Longridge, he made another survey of the
passengers, and, after waiting until the station had
been cleared, he went into the Railway Station Hotel,
searched all the places on the ground-floor, then went
and made a tour of inspection over the adjoining
grounds, but being apparently unsuccessful, trotted
back to the train, and took his old position just as it
was moving off. On reaching the station from which
he had first started, he again looked round as before,
and took his departure. It seems that he now proceeded to the general railway station at Preston, and,
after repeating the looking round performance, placed
himself under one of the seats in a train which he had
singled out of the many that are constantly popping in
and out, and in due time arrived at Liverpool. He
now visited a few places where he had before been
with his master, of whom, as it afterwards appeared,
he was in search. Of his adventures in Liverpool little
is known, but he remained over night, and visited
Preston again early the following morning. Still not
finding his missing master, he for the fourth time
"took the train," this time, however, to Lancaster and
Carlisle, at which latter place the sagacity and faithfulness of the animal, as well as the perseverance and
tact he displayed in prosecuting his search, were
rewarded by finding his master. Their joy at meeting
was mutual.

19. We are told by Plutarch of a certain Roman slave in the civil wars, whose head nobody durst cut off, for fear of the dog that guarded his body, and fought in his defence. It happened that King Pyrrhus, travelling that way, observed the animal watching over the body of the deceased, and hearing that he had been there three days without meat or drink, yet would not forsake his master, ordered the body to be buried, and the dog preserved and brought to him. A few days afterwards, there was a muster of the soldiers, so that every man was forced to march in order before the king. The dog lay quietly by him for some time; but when he saw the murderers of his late owner pass by, he flew upon them with extraordinary fury, barking, and tearing their garments, and frequently turning about to the king, which both excited the king's suspicion, and the jealousy of all who stood about him. The men were in consequence apprehended, and though the circumstances which appeared in evidence against them were very slight, they confessed the crime, and were accordingly punished.

20. A gentleman named Macaire, an officer of the king's body-guard, entertained, for some reason, a bitter hatred against another gentleman, named Aubrey de Montdidier, his comrade in service. These two having met in the Forest of Bondis, near Paris, Macaire took an opportunity of treacherously murdering his brother officer, and buried him in a ditch. Montdidier was unaccompanied at the moment, excepting by a greyhound, with which he had probably gone out to hunt. It is not known whether the dog was

muzzled, or from what other cause it permitted the
deed to be accomplished without its interference. Be
this as it might, the hound lay down on the grave of
its master, and there remained till hunger compelled
it to rise. It then went to the kitchen of one of Aubrey
de Montdidier's dearest friends, where it was welcomed
warmly, and fed. As soon as its hunger was appeased
the dog disappeared. For several days this coming
and going was repeated, till at last the curiosity of
those who saw its movements was excited, and it was
resolved to follow the animal, and see if anything
could be learned in explanation of Montdidier's sudden
disappearance. The dog was accordingly followed, and
was seen to come to a pause on some newly turned up
earth, where it set up the most mournful wailings and
howlings. These cries were so touching, that passengers were attracted, and finally digging into the ground
at the spot, they found there the body of Aubrey de
Montdidier. It was raised and conveyed to Paris,
where it was soon afterwards interred in one of the
city cemeteries. The dog attached itself from this
time forth to the friend, already mentioned, of its late
master. While attending on him, it chanced several
times to get a sight of Macaire, and on every occasion
it sprang upon him and would have strangled him, had
it not been taken off by force. This intensity of hate
on the part of the animal awakened a suspicion that
Macaire had had some share in Montdidier's murder,
for his body showed him to have met a violent death.
Charles V., on being informed of the circumstances,
wished to satisfy himself of their truth. He caused

Macaire and the dog to be brought before him, and beheld the animal again spring upon the object of its hatred. The king interrogated Macaire closely, but the latter would not admit that he had been in any way connected with Montdidier's murder. Being strongly impressed by a conviction, that the conduct of the dog was based on some guilty act of Macaire, the king ordered a combat to take place between the officer and his dumb accuser, according to the practice, in those days, between human plaintiffs and defendants. This remarkable combat took place on the Isle of Notre Dame, at Paris, in presence of the whole court. The king allowed Macaire to have a strong club as a defensive weapon, while, on the other hand, the only self-preservative means allowed to the dog, consisted of an empty cask, into which it could retreat if hard pressed. The combatants appeared in the lists. The dog seemed perfectly aware of its situation and duty. For a short time it leapt actively around Macaire, and then, at one spring, it fastened itself upon his throat in so firm a manner that he could not disentangle himself. He would have been strangled had he not cried for mercy, and avowed his crime. The dog was pulled from off him, but he was only liberated from its fangs to perish by the hands of the law. The fidelity of this 'dog has been celebrated in many a drama and poem, and it has been usually called the Dog of Montargis, from the combat having taken place at the chateau of Montargis.

21. My own experience furnishes me with an instance, like the preceding ones, of the dog. I had, many years ago, a Newfoundland dog, as thoroughly

attached to me as these faithful creatures generally are to those who use them well. It became inconvenient for me to keep him, and I gave him to one who I knew would be kind to him. Four years passed, and I had not seen him, although I had often inquired about him; but one day I was walking towards Kingston, and had arrived at the brow of the hill, where Jerry Abershaw's gibbet then stood, when I met Carlo and the master to whom I had consigned him. He recollected me in a moment, and we made much of each other. His master, after a little chat, proceeded towards Wandsworth, and Carlo, as in duty bound, followed him. I had not, however, got more than half way down the hill, when he was by my side, lowly but deeply growling, and every hair bristling. I looked at the right, and there were two ill looking fellows making their way through the bushes, which then occupied the angular space between the Roehampton and Wandsworth roads. Their intention was scarcely questionable, and, indeed a week or two before, I had narrowly escaped from two miscreants like them. I can scarcely tell what I felt, for, presently, one of the scoundrels emerged from the bushes not twenty yards from me; but he no sooner saw my companion, and heard his growling, the loudness and depth of which were fearfully increasing, than he retreated, and I saw no more of him or of his associate. My gallant defender accompanied me to the direction post at the bottom of the hill, and there, with many a mutual and honest greeting we parted, and he bounded awsy to overtake his rightful owner. We never met again;

but I need not say that I often thought of him with admiration and gratitude.

22. The attachment of the dog remains long after the death of the master, and in some cases, terminates only with the existence of the quadruped. A gentleman having lost his way in a fog near the Helvellyn mountains, in Cumberland, fell down a precipice, and was dashed to pieces. The remains were discovered full three months afterwards, at the bottom, still guarded by his faithful dog. The story is told with much feeling by Sir Walter Scott:—

"Dark was the spot 'mid the brown mountain heather,
Where the pilgrim of nature lay stretched in decay;
Like the corpse of an outcast abandoned to weather,
Till the mountain winds wasted the tenantless clay,
Yet, not quite deserted, though lonely extended,
For, faithful in death, his mute favourite attended,
The much lov'd remains of his master defended,
And chased the hill-fox and the raven away."

23. A butcher had such implicit dependance on the attention of his dog to his orders, that whenever he put a lot of sheep before her, he took a pride in leaving them entirely to her, and either remained to take a glass with the farmer from whom he made the purchase, or went another road to look after other bargains. But one time he chanced to commit a drove to her charge without attending to her condition, as he ought to have done. His farm was five miles away over the wild hills, and there was no regularly defined path to it. On coming home late in the evening, he was astonished to hear that his faithful animal had not made her appearance with the flock. He and his son immediately prepared to set out in different directions in search of

her; but, on their getting into the lane, there she was,
coming with the drove, and not one missing; but she
carrying a young pup in her mouth. She had been
taken in travail on those hills, and how the poor beast
had contrived to manage the drove in her state of
suffering, is beyond human calculation, for her road
lay through sheep the whole way. Her master's heart
smote him when he saw what she had suffered and
effected; but she was nothing daunted, and having
deposited her young one in a place of safety, she again
set out at full speed to the hills, and brought another,
and another, until she had removed her whole litter,
one by one. The last one was dead.

24. Another person had more upon his conscience,
for he, not sufficiently regarding the situation of his
dog, took her nearly twenty miles from home, and she
gave birth to her young at almost the greatest distance
She also brought her offspring home, one by one, but
they were all dead; and when she arrived with the
last one, she had just strength enough remaining to
crawl to her bed, and she looked wistfully in her
master's face, and died.

25. Of the staunchness and incorruptible fidelity of
the dog, the following anecdote is an illustration. An
officer of Holstein returned from a day's shooting
extremely fatigued. He hastily placed the game in his
chamber, locked the door, and unconsciously shut in
his dogs. He was almost immediately afterwards dispatched on business, and departed, forgetting his game.
He was absent many days. On his return, he hastened
to his chamber, where he found the faithful dogs

stretched by the side of the game, and dead. Several partridges and hares were strewed around them, but they had not touched one of them, nor had they cried to be released, which would have been immediately heard in the chateau, because they imagined that they were placed there by their master to guard the produce of their day's excursion.

26. A friend of mine possessed a water-dog of nearly the same breed, which evinced a degree of intelligence scarcely less than human. One instance of her sagacity and faithfulness I cannot refuse myself the pleasure of recording. My friend was travelling on the Continent, and his faithful dog was his companion. One day, before he left his lodgings in the morning, with the expectation of being absent until evening, he took out his purse in his room for the purpose of ascertaining whether he had taken sufficient money for a day's occupation, and then went his way, leaving his dog behind. Having dined at a coffee-house, he took out his purse, and missed a *louis d'or*, searched for it diligently, but to no purpose. Returning home in the evening, his servant let him in, with a face of much sorrow, and told him that the poor dog was very ill, as she had not eaten anything all day, and what appeared very strange, she would not suffer him to take her food away from before her, but had been lying with her nose close to the vessel without attempting to touch it. On my friend entering his room, she instantly jumped upon him, then laid the *louis d'or* at his feet, and immediately began to devour her food with great voracity. The truth was now apparent: my

2 D

friend had dropped the money in the morning when
leaving his room, and the faithful creature finding it,
had held it in her mouth, until his return enabled her
to restore it to his own hands—even refusing to eat
for a whole day, lest it should be out of her custody.
I knew the dog well, and have witnessed very many
curious tricks of hers showing docility.

27. I have a poodle whom I would make tutor to my
son, if I had one, I sometimes use him towards my
own education. Will not the following trait of his
character amuse you? He conceived a strange fondness, an absolute passion, for a young kitten, which
he carried about in his mouth for hours when
he went out to walk, and whenever he came to a
resting-place, he set her down with the greatest care
and tenderness, and began to play with her. When he
was fed, she·always took the nicest pieces away from
him, without his ever making the slighest opposition.
The kitten died, and was buried in the garden. My
poor poodle showed the deepest grief, would not touch
food, and howled mournfully the whole night long.
What was my astonishment, when, the next morning,
he appeared carrying the kitten in his mouth! He had
scratched her out of the ground, and it was only by
force that we could take her from him.

28. Our post-master has a strangely sagacious dog. A
great deal of business is done at the post-office, and a
great many messages dispatched from it to the various
villages. The dog, Charlie, sits at the front door of a
morning, and signals, by a short bark, as each individual
messenger rounds the corner into the street: the short

bark is sufficient to tell the clerk in the office that his attention will be required. So soon as the milkman appears, Charlie runs in-doors with a loud continuous bow-wow, as it is uncertain in what part of the house the person may be who should attend the " milky way." Charlie knows me well, and shows marked fondness for me, but he always barks at my approach on Sunday mornings.

29. Smut, a town mendicant, got his living in a safe way. He was a black shaggy spaniel, of average size, who, with a little attention, might have been accounted handsome, and he was generally supposed to have a master, though in reality he had none. He knew, and was known to, nearly all the city dining houses, which he would enter at dining hours, and there beg for bones and scraps among the customers. He had the precaution to limit his stay at one place to about half an hour at the most, and as the waiters invariably supposed his master to be present, he rarely encountered any opposition from them. Several attempts were made by those who knew him to attach him to themselves and give him a permanent home, but none of them succeeded. Smut preferred a nomadic life; and though he would stay for a day or two with an indulgent patron, he invariably ended by asserting his independence, and resumed his vagabond mendicant life. It was said that he finally fell a victim to the police, who, finding him airing his tongue one sweltering day in August, sacrificed him to the dog-star and the Lord Mayor's proclamation against hydrophobia.

30. In the course of last summer, it chanced that
the sheep on the farm of a friend of ours, on the water
of Stinchar, were, like those of his neighbours, partially
affected with a common disease in the skin, to cure
which distemper it is necessary to cut off the wool
over the part affected, and apply a small quantity of
balsam.  For this purpose, the shepherd set off to the
hill one morning, accompanied by his faithful canine
assistant, Laddie.  Arrived among the flock, the shepherd pointed out a diseased animal, and making the
accustomed signal for the dog to capture it, "poor
Mailie" was speedily sprawling on her back, and gently
held down by the dog till the arrival of her keeper,
who proceeded to clip off a portion of her wool, and
apply the healing balsam.  During the operation,
Laddie continued to gaze on the operator with close
attention, and the sheep having been released, he was
directed to capture in succession two or three more of
the flock, which underwent similar treatment.  The
sagacious animal had now become initiated into the
mysteries of his master's vocation, for off he set unbidden through the flock, and picked out with unerring
precision those sheep which were affected, and held
them down until the arrival of his master, who was
thus, by the extraordinary instinct of Laddie, saved a
world of trouble, while the operation of clipping and
smearing was also greatly facilitated.

31. Domestic animals not unfrequently contract sudden fancies for, and occasionally as sudden aversions to
particular individuals, in a strange manner, the latter
being apparently more difficult to understand than the

former. Doubtless something or other has passed
through the animal's mind, which, could we know what
it was, would fully account for this conduct on their
part, while to those unacquainted with the cause, they
appear to be actuated solely by caprice. The following
instances have happened to occur within my own
knowledge. A brother of mine, when in the army, had
a very favourite little spaniel which was devotedly
attached to him, and his constant companion. During
a visit of a few days however, which I paid him, when
quartered at Cork, and on the eve of embarkation for
foreign service, the dog took such an extraordinary
fancy for me, that he decidedly preferred my company
to that of my brother, and indeed quite deserted him
for me. On my leaving to return to England, my
brother kindly gave him to me, and he, as a matter of
course, followed me on board the steamer, leaving my
brother standing on the quay. The steamer sheered off,
and proceeded on her course; but no sooner did the
dog perceive that he was really to be separated from his
old master, than all his former affection for him appeared
to return in its full force; in every way in which a dog
can express contrition, he seemed to do so for his error
in having forsaken him for me; and I was actually
obliged to hold him, in order to prevent him from jumping overboard to rejoin him. I had poor Brick for some
years afterwards until one unlucky day when, during my
absence from home, he was taken out rabbit shooting by
the servants, and a stray shot ended his existence.

32. Having alluded to my little dog "Brick," I cannot
refrain, before taking leave of him here, from men-

tioning the original method in which he used to
resent the impertinences of a small cur, which was con-
tinually insulting his dignity by running up and barking
at him. When this happened, Brick used to " go in "
at the offender, as if determined to chastise him, which
he would perhaps have done, had not the other at once
cried " peccavi," and deprecated his wrath by lying down
crouching on his back. I have read of a big dog under
similar circumstances taking up the smaller one, and
dropping him into a dirty puddle.

33. Two other of his peculiarities, may, perhaps, be
also worth recording. One of these was his extreme
sensitiveness in point of " ear " for music. If he were
lying asleep in the drawing-room, and two or three
discords were purposely struck on the piano, he would
instantly jump up and express his horror of them by
a dismal whine. The other, was his dislike to have
anything floating about in his " tea." I have seen him
start back and growl at a tea twig (in nursery parlance
" stranger ") which happened to come to the surface
whilst he was drinking it.

34. The following I have from an old and much
valued friend, a good and scientific naturalist:—" Walking with a favourite Newfoundland dog of great size,
one frosty day, he observed the animal's repeated
disappointment on putting his head down, with the
intention to drink, at sundry ice-covered pools. After
one of these disappointments, my friend broke the ice
with his foot, for his thirsty companion's behoof. The
next time it seemed good to the dog to try and drink,
instead of waiting for his master to break the ice as

before, he set his own huge paw forcibly on the ice, and, with a little effort, obtained water for himself.

35. Dogs perform an important part in street-begging in London. They have been known, on the receipt of a penny, to run to the baker's shop, and bring their master a piece of bread. We have read of a dog, who, on the death of his blind master, followed up his old calling by begging on his own account. Another instance of canine wit, which seems to have a smack of the facetious in it, is that of a dog who made a living by shoe-blacking in Paris. The animal, in his desire to serve his master, would roll into the gutter for the purpose of throwing mud upon the shoes of pedestrians. The following is the account quoted from Chambers :—An English officer, who was in Paris in 1815, mentions the case of a dog belonging to a shoe-black, which brought customers to its master. This it did in a very ingenious, and scarcely honest manner. The officer, having occasion to cross one of the bridges over the Seine, had his boots, which had been previously polished, dirtied by a poodle-dog rubbing against them. He, in consequence, went to a man who was stationed on the bridge, and had them cleaned. The same circumstance having occurred more than once, his curiosity was excited, and he watched the dog. He saw him roll himself into the mud of the river, and then watch for a person with well polished boots, against which he contrived to rub himself. Finding that the shoe-black was the owner of the dog, he taxed him with the artifice; and, after a little hesitation, he confessed that he had taught the dog the trick, in

order, to procure customers for himself. The officer, being much struck with the dog's sagacity, purchased him at a high price, and brought him to England. He kept him tied up in London some time, and then released him. The dog remained with him a day or two, and then made his escape. A fortnight afterwards, he was found with his former master, pursuing his old trade of dirtying gentlemen's boots on the bridge. Instances of the strong attachment of the beggar's dog may often be witnessed. Not only does he enact the guide to the blind, but he performs other services equally essential; taking up the alms dropped for his mendicant master, or holding a cup to receive the contributions of the charitable. And often is he seen placing himself in an erect attitude, with a most beseeching visage, which tells well upon the pocket.

36. A gentleman was missed in London, and was supposed to have met with some foul play. No clue could be obtained to the mystery, till it was gained from observing his dog continue to crouch down before a certain house. The animal would not be induced to leave the spot, and it was at length inferred that he might be waiting for his master. The house, hitherto above suspicion, was searched, and the result was the discovery of the body of the missing individual, who had been murdered. The guilty parties were arrested, confessed their crime; and thus one of the "dens of London" was broken up by the "police knowledge" of this faithful dog.

37. Our superintendent of police had a dog, Toby, which he had given to a friend in a neighbouring town.

Mr. Superintendent H. drove through the town some months after, and as he came into the inn-yard, some one hundred and fifty yards from where the dog as, and out of sight of the late owner, the person said, there's Mr. —— just gone into the —— Arms. Up jumped Toby, and ran off immediately to his old master's quarters, and began to testify the customary joyous recognition.

38. A mansion in Gloucestershire had been let to a new family who undertook not only to keep the house in order, but to maintain a large dog which had been left there by the owner of the house. When the new comers went away for the season, the dog was placed on board wages with the dairy maid, who is supposed not to have over fed her boarder, and therefore at all future breakings up of the establishment, he knew by preparatory packing and other signs that the day of dearth was approaching, and very wisely used to prepare for famine, by hoarding up unpicked bones and all scraps, which he would at other times, and in palmy days, have turned up his nose at.

39. In the triumphal entrance of the troops here, the heroes of the day, (with the exception of General Prim, who was so greeted that he had to deliver half a dozen speeches as he went through the streets,) were a trumpeter and a dog. Their glory obscured that of all the army, and they obtained an ovation which will disturb the repose of Espartero at Logrono. The trumpeter belongs to the Bourbon regiment; he is only fourteen years, and is of short stature. When in Africa, he happened, one day, whilst

in the advanced posts with his company, to be exces-
sively hungry, and he could not get any food. At last
he perceived a number of oak trees, and said to himself,
" Where there are oak trees there are acorns, which at
a pinch can be eaten !" He accordingly slipped away,
and passed unobserved by the sentinels, climbed up
the tree and began eating. He was suddenly interrupted by a strange noise, and to his dismay, perceived
that the tree was surrounded by furious looking Moors.
Flight was impossible, and resistance out of the question ; but a bright idea struck him : he seized his
trumpet and sounded the charge. The Moors thinking
that they had fallen into an ambush, took to flight.
This exploit of the trumpeter excited great admiration
at the time, and on the entrance of the troops, the
crowd not only greeted him with enthusiasm, but he
was borne in triumph on men's shoulders, and crowned
with laurel ! From time to time, at the request of the
people, he sounded the charge which had struck terror
into the breasts of the Moors. As to the dog, he belongs to the riflemen of Baza. He was sold by his
owner for a loaf, to a soldier of the 4th company, at
Barcelona ; and his new master gave him the name of
Palomo, and shared with him his food. The other
soldiers also treated him kindly, and the animal conceived an affection not only for his master but for the
whole of the men. When the war broke out, the
battalion was ordered to Algesiras to embark, and the
dog was left behind at Barcelona. But just as the
battalion was about to leave, he reached that port and
joined the men ; how he found his way there, none

could tell. He was, however, left behind; but one day he arrived mysteriously in Morocco, and again joined his battalion! He took part in all the combats up to the taking of Tetuan, and in that affair he was struck by a ball, which has made him lame for life. In the entrance of the troops, he marched modestly at the head of his battalion, but was covered with flowers and laurel. He has been appointed honorary corporal in the battalion, and wore the insignia of that grade.

40. A dog belonging to a celebrated chemist, had tried upon it the effects of a certain poison, and upon the next day a counter-poison was administered with the effect of preserving the creature's life. The following day another dose was offered him, but he would not touch it. Different sorts of poisonous drugs were presented to him, but he resolutely refused all; bread was offered, but he would not touch it; meat, but he turned from it; water, but he would not drink. To reassure him, his master offered him bread and meat of which he himself ate in the dog's presence, and of that the sagacious animal hesitated not to partake. He was then taken to a fountain, but he would drink nowhere but from the spot where the water gushed free and fresh. This continued for several days, until the master touched by the extraordinary intelligence of the poor creature, resolved to make no more attempts upon him with his poisons.

41. A dog having been given by a gentlemen of Wivenhoe to the captain of a collier, he took the dog on board his vessel, and landed with him at Sunderland. But soon after his arrival there, the dog was

missing, and in a very few days arrived at the residence of his old master in Essex.

42. A still more extraordinary circumstance is upon record, of the late Colonel Hardy, who being sent for express to Bath, was accompanied by a favourite spaniel in his chaise, which he never quitted till his arrival there. After remaining there four days, he accidentally left his spaniel behind, and returned to his residence at Springfield in Essex, with equal expedition, where, in three days after, his faithful and steady adherent arrived also, notwithstanding the distance between that place and Bath is one hundred and forty miles; and she had to explore her way through London, to which she had never been, but in her passage to Bath, and then within the confines of a close carriage.

43. A few years ago, the public were amused with an account given in the newspapers of a dog which pos· sessed the strange fancy of attending all the fires that occurred in the metropolis   The discovery of this predilection was made by a gentleman residing a few miles from town, who was called up in the middle of the night by the intelligence that the premises adjoining his house of business were on fire. " The removal of my books and papers," said he, in telling the story, " of course claimed my attention ; yet, notwithstanding this, and the bustle which prevailed, my eye every now and then rested on a dog, whom, during the hottest progress of the conflagration, I could not help noticing running about, and apparently taking a deep interest in what was going on, contriving to keep out of every

body's way, and yet always present amidst the thickest
of the stir. When the fire was got under, and I had
leisure to look about me, I again observed the dog,
which, with the firemen, appeared to be resting from
the fatigues of duty, and was led to make some inquiries
respecting him. ' Is this your dog, my friend?' said I
to a fireman. ' No, sir,' answered he; 'it does not
belong to me, or to any one in particular. We call him
the firemen's dog.' ' The firemen's dog!' I replied.
' Why so? Has he no master?' ' No, sir,' rejoined the
fireman; ' he calls none of us master, though we are all
of us willing enough to give him a night's lodging and
a pennyworth of meat. But he wont stay long with
any of us; his delight is to be at all the fires in London;
and, far or near, we generally find him on the road as
we are going along, and sometimes, if it is out of town,
we give him a lift. I don't think there has been a fire
for these two or three years past which he has not
been at.' The communication was so extraordinary
that I found it difficult to believe the story, until it was
confirmed by the concurrent testimony of several other
firemen. None of them, however, were able to give any
account of the early habits of the dog, or to offer any
explanation of the circumstances which led to this
singular propensity. Some time afterwards, I was
again called up in the night to a fire in the village in
which I resided (Camberwell, in Surrey), and to my
surprise here I again met with ' the firemen's dog, still
alive and well, pursuing, with the same apparent interest and satisfaction, the exhibition of that which
seldom fails to bring with it disaster and misfortune,

E

oftentimes loss of life and ruin. Still, he called no
man master, disdained to receive bed or board from
the same hand more than a night or two at a time, nor
could the firemen trace out his resting-place" Such
was the account of this interesting animal as it
appeared in the newspapers, to which were shortly
afterwards appended several circumstances communicated by a fireman at one of the police-offices. A
magistrate having asked him whether it was a fact that
the dog was present at most of the fires that occurred
in the metropolis, the fireman replied that he never
knew "Tyke," as he was called, to be absent from a
fire upon any occasion that he [the fireman] attended
himself. The magistrate said the dog must have an
extraordinary predilection for fires. He then asked
what length of time he had been known to possess that
propensity. The fireman replied that he knew Tyke
for the last nine years; and although he was getting
old, yet the moment the engines were about, Tyke was
to be seen as active as ever, running off in the direction
of the fire. The magistrate inquired whether the dog
lived with any particular fireman. The fireman replied
that Tyke liked one fireman as well as another; he had
no particular favourites, but passed his time amongst
them, sometimes going to the house of one, and then
to another, and off to a third when he was tired. Day
or night, it was all the same to him; if a fire broke out,
there he was in the midst of the bustle, running from
one engine to another, anxiously looking after the
firemen; and, although pressed upon by crowds, yet,
from his dexterity, he always escaped accidents, only

now and then getting a ducking from the engines, which he rather liked than otherwise. The magistrates said that Tyke was a most extraordinary animal, and having expressed a wish to see him, he was shortly after exhibited at the office, and some other peculiarites respecting him were related. There was nothing at all particular in the appearance. He was a rough-looking small animal, of the terrier breed, and seemed to be in excellent condition, no doubt from the care taken of him by the firemen belonging to the different companies. There was some difficulty experienced in bringing him to the office, as he did not much relish going any distance from where the firemen are usually to be found, except in cases of attending them at a conflagration, and then distance was of no consequence. It was found necessary to use stratagem for the purpose. A fireman commenced running: Tyke, accustomed to follow upon such occasions, set out after him ; but this person having slackened his pace on the way, the sagacious animal, knowing there was no fire, turned back, and it was necessary to carry him to the office.

44. The following striking anecdote of a similar kind appeared in the first number of the new issue of Cassell's Illustrated Family Paper. After giving a short account of a fire-escape man, named Samuel Wood, the writer thus alludes to his dog Bill :—"As to Bill, he regards him evidently in the light of a friend ; he had him when he was a pup, from a poor fellow who died in the service, and he and his 'Bill' have been on excellent terms ever since. The fire

escape man's dog takes after his master in courage and perseverance. He is of a terrier breed, six years old. An alarm of fire calls forth all his energy. He is the first to know something is wrong, the first to exert himself in setting it right. He has not been trained to the work, 'it is a gift,' as his master says; and if we all used our gifts as efficiently as the dog Bill, it would be the better for us. On an alarm of fire, Bill barks his loudest, dashes about in a frantic manner, till his master and the escape are on their way to it. He, of course, is there first, giving the police and the crowd to understand that Wood and his fire-escape are coming. When the escape is fixed, and Wood begins to ascend the ladder, Bill runs up the canvas; as soon as a window is opened, Bill leaps in, and dashes about to find the occupants, loudly barking for assistance as soon as he has accomplished his errand of mercy. His watchfulness and sagacity are never at fault, although on more than one occasion he has stood a fair chance of losing his life, and has sustained very severe injury. Not long ago, a collar was presented to Bill, as a reward for his services; unfortunately for him, he has since lost this token of public regard—a misfortune much to be regretted. The following verse was engraved on the collar :—

"I am the fire-escape man's dog, my name is Bill,
When 'fire' is called, I am never still;
I bark for my master, all danger brave,
So bring the escape—human life to save."

Collared or collarless, Bill is always ready to lend a helping bark. May his life be long, and his services properly esteemed! "

45. A boy at Athens of a very amiable character, had a dog that had been his playmate from his cradle. The animal was so fond of his young master, that he scarcely ever quitted him; he accompanied him in all his sports, and whenever he saw him again after a short absence, he expressed his pleasure by a thousand caresses. He always eat his meals with him, slept at his feet at night, rose with him in the morning, and both began the day playing with each other. One day this young Athenian, looking out of the window at some exhibition that was passing along the street, overreached himself, and losing his balance, fell from the upper story of the house to the ground, and was killed on the spot. Phileros (that was the name of the dog) immediately leaped after him, and broke his leg with the fall. But, occupied wholly with anxiety for his master, he crawled about him, licked him with a mournful howling, and crept under his body, as if to endeavour to raise him from the ground. During the preparation for the funeral, Phileros would not quit the lifeless body of his master, and followed the procession that bore him to the grave. When he came to the place of burial, he set up a lamentable cry, and remained for five days lying upon the grave. Compelled, by his cravings of hunger, he then returned to the house, eat a small quantity of food, after which he ran to the apartment which the child inhabited, seemed to seek everywhere for his young friend, and in a short time died of grief.

46. Dogs have a great deal of jealousy in their disposition, and even this may be made to assist in their

2 E

education, as it makes them strive to outdo each other. Every clever dog is especially unwilling that any of his companions should possess a greater share of his master's favour than himself. One of my dogs could not be induced to hunt in company with another, of whose advances in my good graces he was peculiarly jealous. There was no other ground of quarrel between them. When Rover saw that a young dog was to accompany me, he invariably refused to go out; and, although at other times, one of the most eager dogs for sport that I ever possessed, nothing would induce him to go out with his young rival. He also showed his jealousy by flying at him and biting him, on every occasion when he could do so unobserved. At last, however, when the young dog had grown older, and discovered that his own strength was superior to that of his tyrant, he flew upon poor Rover, and amply revenged all the ill-treatment which he had received at his hands. From that day he was constantly on the look out to renew his attacks; but having soon es tablished his superiority, he thenceforth contented himself with striking down the old dog, and, after standing over him a minute or two, with teeth bared ready for action, he suffered him to sneak quietly away; for Rover was too old a soldier to resist when he found himself over-matched. At last the poor old fellow got so bullied by this dog, and by two or three others, whom I am afraid he had tyrannized over when they were puppies, that he never left the front door steps, or went round the corner of the house, before he had well reconnoitred the ground, and was sure that none of his enemies were near him. And yet, in his battles with vermin or with strange dogs, he was one of the most courageous animals I ever had.

47. Mr. Youatt tells us of a dog which though very ill-tempered and spoiled, so much so that it would not suffer a stranger to touch her, having become diseased, so as to require an operation of a painful kind, which he carefully performed, whenever she saw him afterwards, testified her joy and gratitude in the most expressive and endearing manner.

48. A large Newfoundland dog, that may be seen any day at No. 9, Argyle-street, Glasgow, has added one more instance to the many on record of the sagacity of dogs. It seems that being, like other juveniles, sometimes rather fond of fun, he required to receive occasional discipline, and for that purpose a whip shaft was kept beside him, which was occasionally applied to him. He evidently did not like this article, and was found occasionally with it in his teeth moving slily to the door with it. Being left at night on the premises, he found the hated article, and thrust the small end below the door, but the thick end refused to go. A few nights afterwards the whip shaft was left beside him, and was never seen again. He had put the thick end below the door, and some one had pulled it out. On the dog being asked where it was, he looked very guilty, and slunk away with his tail between his legs. This same dog gets his provisions brought to him in a tin can. Taking a walk, he saw a child carrying a tin exceedingly like his. He quietly seized it by the handle and carried it to his quarters, the child holding

on and screaming all the way. When shown his own, he seemed quite ashamed of his mistake, and allowed the frightened child to go with the tin he had mistaken for his own. This sagacious dog is in the habit of begging money from his biped acquaintance, with which he marches to a baker's shop and buys bread, which he comes home with, and eats when hungry.

49. Extraordinary as the following anecdote may appear, it is strictly true, and shows the sense, and I am strongly inclined to add, reason, of the Newfoundland dog:—A friend of mine, while shooting wildfowl with his brother, was attended by a sagacious dog of this breed. In getting near some reeds by the side of a river, they threw down their hats, and crept to the edge of the water, where they fired at some birds. They soon afterwards sent the dog to bring their hats, one of which was smaller than the other. After several attempts to bring them both together in his mouth, the dog at last placed the smaller hat in the larger one, pressed it down with his foot, and thus was able to bring them both at the same time.

50. Mr. Charles O'Neil, shoemaker, Stackstead, owns a favourite dog, which is so knowing, that it is only necessary to tell him to go to the shop of Mr. Cox, news-agent, for the newspaper, and away it goes. If the door be closed, the dog keeps rapping at it until it is opened; and on the newspaper being presented, he takes it in his mouth, wags his tail, and off he goes again to his master. The dog has never been known to let the money drop when sent for the newspaper.

51. A somewhat curious example of intelligence in a dog, is stated to have occurred a few days ago, at Toulouse. Some mischievous boys fastened a tin kettle to its tail, and the poor animal, in great terror, ran off, closely pursued by them. In spite of his terror, the dog, it was noticed, looked in a peculiar way at the houses he passed, as if seeking for shelter in one of them; and at last, seeing one in which was the office of commissary of police, he rushed into it, entered the office, and quietly lay down, as if certain of obtaining protection. If the local newspapers are to be believed, the reason why the dog selected the office of the commissary, in preference to any other, was, that his mistress, an old and somewhat eccentric lady, having a few days before, been persecuted by the same boys, went to the commissary, and sought and obtained his protection. The dog, which was with her at the time, remembered, the local journals remark, the effect produced, and in his turn took advantage of it.

52. Fidelity to the interests of his master is one of the most pleasing traits in the character of the dog, and could be exemplified by so many anecdotes, that the difficulty consists in making a proper selection. The following, however, is worthy of commendation :—A French merchant having some money due from a correspondent, set out on horseback, accompanied by his dog, on purpose to receive it. Having settled the business to his satisfaction, he tied the bag of money before him, and began to return home. His faithful dog, as if he entered into his master's feelings, frisked round the horse, barked, and jumped, and seemed to participate

in his joy. The merchant, after riding some miles,
alighted to repose himself under an agreeable shade,
and taking the bag of money in his hand, laid it down
by his side under a hedge, and on remounting, forgot
it. The dog perceived his lapse of recollection, and
wishing to rectify it, ran to fetch the bag; but it was
too heavy for him to drag along. He ran to his master,
and by crying, barking, and howling, seemed to remind
him of his mistake. The merchant understood not his
language; but the assiduous creature persevered in its
efforts, and after trying to stop the horse in vain, at last
began to bite his heels. The merchant, absorbed in
some reverie, wholly overlooked the real object of his
affectionate attendant's importunity, but entertained
the alarming apprehension that he was gone mad. Full
of this suspicion, in crossing a brook, he turned back to
look if the dog would drink. The animal was too intent
on his master's business to think of itself; it continued
to bark and bite with greater violence than before. "It
must be so," cried the afflicted merchant, "my poor dog
is certainly mad: what must I do? I must kill him,
lest some greater misfortune befal me; but with what
regret! Oh could I find any one to perform this cruel
office for me! But there is no time to lose; I myself
may become the victim if I spare him." With these
words he drew a pistol from his pocket, and with a
trembling hand took aim at his faithful servant. He
turned away in agony as he fired; but his aim was too
sure. The poor animal fell wounded, and, weltering in
his blood, still endeavoured to crawl towards his master,
as if to tax him with ingratitude. The merchant could

not bear the sight; he spurred on his horse with a heart full of sorrow, and lamented he had taken a journey which had cost him so dear. Still, however, the money never entered his mind; he only thought of his poor dog, and tried to console himself with the reflection that he had prevented a greater evil by despatching a mad animal, than he had suffered a calamity by his loss. This opiate to his wounded spirit, however, was ineffectual: "I am most unfortunate," said he to himself; "'I had almost rather have lost my money than my dog." Saying this, he stretched out his hand to grasp his treasure. It was missing; no bag was to be found. In an instant he opened his eyes to his rashness and folly. "Wretch that I am! I alone am to blame! I could not comprehend the admonition which my innocent and most faithful friend gave me, and I have sacrificed him for his zeal. He only wished to inform me of my mistake, and he paid for his fidelity with his life." Instantly he turned his horse, and went off at full gallop to the place where he had stopped. He saw with half-averted eyes the scene where the tragedy was acted; he perceived the traces of blood as he proceeded; he was oppressed and distracted; but in vain did he look for his dog; he was not to be seen on the road. At last he arrived at the spot where he had alighted. But what were his sensations! His heart was ready to bleed; he execrated himself in the madness of dispair. The poor dog, unable to follow his dear but cruel master, had determined to consecrate his last moments to his service. He had crawled, all bloody as he was, to the forgotten bag, and, in the

agonies of death, he lay watching beside it. When he
saw his master, he still testified his joy by the wagging
of his tale. He could do no more; he tried to rise, but
his strength was gone. The vital tide was ebbing fast;
even the caresses of his master could not prolong his
fate for a few moments. He stretched out his tongue
to lick the hand that was now fondling him in the
agonies of regret, as if to seal forgiveness of the
deed that had deprived him of life. He then cast a
look of kindness on his master, and closed his eyes in
death.

53. A less tragical instance of this kind of fidelity
occurred some years ago in England. A gentleman of
Suffolk, on an excursion with his friend, was attended
by a Newfoundland dog, which soon became the subject
of conversation. The master, after a warm eulogium
upon the perfections of his canine favourite, assured
his companion that he would, upon receiving the order,
return and fetch any article he should leave behind,
from any distance. To confirm this assertion, a marked
shilling was put under a large square stone by the side
of the road—being first shown to the dog. The gentlemen then rode for three miles, when the dog received
his signal from the master to return for the shilling he
had seen put under the stone. The dog turned back;
the gentlemen rode on, and reached home; but, to their
surprise and disappointment, the hitherto faithful messenger did not return during the day. It afterwards
appeared that he had gone to the place where the
shilling was deposited, but the stone being too large
for his strength to remove, he had stayed howling at

the place, till two horsemen riding by, and attracted by his seeming distress, stopped to look at him, when one of them alighting, removed the stone, and seeing the shilling, put it into his pocket, not at the time conceiving it to be the object of the dog's search. The dog followed their horses for twenty miles, remained undisturbed in the room where they supped, followed the chambermaid into the bedchamber, and secreted himself under one of the beds. The possessor of the shilling hung his trousers upon a nail by the bedside; but when the travellers were both asleep, the dog took them in his mouth, and leaping out of the window, which was left open on account of the sultry heat, reached the house of his master at four o'clock in the morning with the prize he had made free with, in the pocket of which were found a watch and money, that were returned upon being advertised, when the whole mystery was mutually unravelled, to the admiration of all the parties.

54. As an instance of generous revenge on the part of this noble creature, there is a story of a person, who, being desirous of getting rid of his dog, took it along with him in a boat, and rowing out into the river Seine, threw it overboard. The poor animal repeatedly struggled to regain the boat, but was as often beaten off; till at length, in his attempts to baffle the efforts of the dog, the man upset the boat, and fell into the water. No sooner, however, did the generous brute see his master struggle in the stream, than he forsook the boat, and held him above water till assistance arrived, and thus saved his life. Was not this dog

morally superior to his owner, in thus returning good for evil?

55. The Rev. Mr. S , an intimate friend of my venerated father, who resided about two miles from Edinburgh, had a dog named Blucher. Blucher was a noble animal. Many a story have I heard about his marvellous deeds. One or two may be deemed worthy of perpetual record. Mr. S. and family, on a certain Lord's Day in summer, had occasion to be absent at Holy Communion from morning till evening. One servant girl and Blucher were left in charge of the house. The girl, availing herself of the absence of the family, invited a number of her associates to spend the day with her. Forenoon and afternoon passed rapidly away, and the godless party gathered amusement from " parlour, garden, green." During all their goings to and fro, Blucher was their faithful attendant. In due time, the company assembled for tea in the drawing-room, on the second story of the house. The lady of the mansion for the time presided at the table, amidst the gay decorations of her mistress' best china, urn, and silver. As the evening sun goes down, the party bethink themselves of retiring, ere Mr. S. and family return. But, lo! the indignant Blucher, who had till now rested himself upon the rug, marches to the door. There he takes up his position, and will not suffer it to be opened. With wrathful eye and growl he beats back every assailant; and the whole company are kept in durance vile till Mr. and Mrs. S. enter upon the scene. The table furniture and ware at once proclaim the story of the day. On seeing his master, Blucher is in a moment

peaceful as a lamb, and delivers up his prisoners with all the high dignity becoming his nobility and worth.

56. In the front of Mr. S.'s house, there was a parterre in which were reared some beautiful flowers. The little children from some cottages in the neigh- bourhood were accustomed to steal in at the gate and pluck the flowers, to the great grief of Mr. and Mrs. S. One day, a little fellow was busy at the work. Blucher espied him, and with a bound was at his side. Gently tossing him down, and turning him on his face, the hero seized the astonished depredator by the clothes which covered his back. Then trotting off with him, he went out at the gate, and passed along the highway till he came to a shallow pool of muddy water, into which he suddenly dropped the delinquent. Making sure that the little fellow was neither hurt nor likely to be drowned, Blucher forthwith went quietly home. The tidings spread amongst the children, and after that memorable day not a flower was ever touched.

57. In course of time, Mr. S. and family had the prospect of removing to a house in the city. They saw it would be somewhat inconvenient to keep Blucher in the abode to which they were going. Still they had no idea of parting with him. One evening Blucher was lying on the hearth before the fire. The family were talking of their removal. Mr. S. said, looking at the dog, "Poor Blucher, what will become of you?" Blucher lifted up his head, as he heard the unusual tones of his master's voice. "Do with me, dear master;" he seemed to say; "What strange sad tones are these!" Shortly after, he left the room, and not-

withstanding every effort within the compass of their
power to discover his retreat, the family never saw or
heard of Blucher more! His loss affected them almost
like the loss of a beloved friend.

58. One other anecdote,—not of Blucher, however,—
but of a fine animal named Help. I tell the tale without
comment, as it was related to me. I knew the family
well, of whose ancestor it speaks. Help belonged to a
farmer at H. Mr. W. had occasion to go to a country
town in a neighbouring district. The road lay for some
miles over a bleak howling wilderness, called Kingside
Edge. The upper ridge of the waste was a noted place
for dangers of different kinds. In the days when Mr.
W. lived there were no railways, not even stage coaches,
and no Banks; at least, there were none of these in the
upland district of P. Mr. W. left home at early dawn,
went over the ridge by a bridle-road on horseback,
reached the county town—where we leave him for a
little, transacting his business within the parlour of an
inn. ' " What's wrong with the dog?" said Mrs. W. at
home, about noon. " He wont be still. He'll tear up
the staple of his chain!" And she gave orders to take
out an extra supply of food for him. Help, however,
would look at neither food nor drink. He bounded
here, and he bounded there, as his chain would allow,
till, at last, Mrs. W., for the peace of the farmyard,
desired him to be loosed, Once free, off he flew by the
way his master went. By this time Mr. W. had finished
his business at P., and was wending his way home. On
nearing the height of the ridge, he saw two men creeping
along behind the hedge. I have seen them before, he

said to himself; and soon he recognized them as two
ruffian-like fellows he had noticed that very morning
within the inn, and who had narrowly watched him
while he was depositing a large sum of money within
his purse. Scarcely had these thoughts passed through
his mind, when out the men started upon the road:
one seized the bridle of his horse, and the other presenting a loaded pistol, demanded his purse. Mr. W.,
on the impulse of the moment, looked around the
waste, and cried out for assistance. "Help, help!" he
shouted; and no sooner were the words uttered, than
he heard a scream from the man with the pistols, and
turning to him, he saw in a moment how the case stood.
To his astonishment, he beheld his own dog, Help, in
conflict with the robber. To strike the man at the
bridle with the heavy end of his whip was now the
work of an instant. The ruffian let go his hold, and
Mr. W. putting spurs to his horse, rode off, and was
soon afar from the scene of danger. Some hours after
he had reached home, Help returned, not a little hurt
and bloody. Mr. W. never heard any tidings of his
assailants; and being a good man, he often talked of
his deliverance as a direct interposition of a kind
Providence in his behalf.

59. A fine Newfoundland dog which was kept at an
inn, in Dorsetshire, was accustomed, every morning, as
the clock struck eight, to take in his mouth a certain
basket, placed for the purpose, and containing a few
pence, and to carry it across the street to the baker's,
who took out the money, and replaced it by a certain
number of rolls; with these Neptune hastened back to

F

the kitchen, and safely deposited his trust. But what was well worthy of remark, he never attempted to take the basket, or even to approach it, on Sunday mornings. On one occasion, when returning with the rolls, another dog made an attack upon the basket, for the purpose of stealing its contents, when the trusty fellow placed the basket on the ground, severely punished the intruder, and then bore off his charge in triumph.

60. A lady living in the neighbourhood of my own village had, some years back, a favourite Scotch terrier, which always accompanied her in her rides, and which was also in the habit of following the carriage to church every Sunday morning. One summer, the lady and her family were from home for several weeks, the dog being left behind. The latter, however, continued to come to church by itself for several Sundays in succession, galloping off from the house so as to arrive at the hour of service commencing. After waiting in the church-yard a short time, it was seen to return, quiet and dispirited, home. The distance from the house to the church is three miles, and beyond that at which the ringing of the bells could be ordinarily heard. This was probably an instance of the force of habit, assisted by some association of recollections connected with the movements of the household on that particular day of the week.

61. The same lady has communicated to me an anecdote, somewhat similar to the above, but more ex-traordinary. This related to a poodle dog belonging to a gentleman in Chester, which it appears was in the habit of not only going to church, but remaining quietly

in the pew during service, whether his master was there or not. One Sunday, the dam at the head of a lake in that neighbourhood gave way, so that the whole road was inundated. The congregation, in consequence, consisted of a few who came from some cottages close by, but nobody attended from the great house. The clergyman informed the lady, that, whilst reading the Psalms, he saw his friend the poodle come slowly up the aisle dripping with wet, having swum about a quarter of a mile to get to church. He went as usual into the pew, and remained to the end of the service.

62. The above lady has also given the following anecdote of a dog and cat. A little Blenheim Spaniel of hers once accompanied her to the house of a relation, where it was taken into the kitchen to be fed, on which occasion two large favourite cats flew at it several times, and scratched it severely. The spaniel was in the habit of following its mistress in her walks in the garden, and, by degrees, it formed a friendship with a young cat of the gardener's, which it tempted into the house, —first into the hall, and then into the kitchen,—where, on finding one of the large cats, the spaniel and its ally fell on it together, and without further provocation beat it well; they then waited for the other, which they served in the same manner, and finally drove both cats from the kitchen. The two friends continued afterwards to eat off the same plate as long as the spaniel remained with her mistress in the house.

63. A King Charles' spaniel belonging to a lady, a relation of my own, was constantly in the habit of attending her when she went out driving, and, if it was

wished that he should not accompany her, it was
necessary to shut him up to prevent him from doing so
On Sundays she went to teach at the village school,
where his presence was of course undesirable.  To my
surprise, one Sunday morning I saw her preparing for a
start to the school, leaving " Beau " at liberty in the
dining-room, which was on the ground-floor, opening on
the carriage drive by which she would leave the house.
I was proceeding to shut him up, when she said, " Oh
you need not trouble yourself to do that, he knows
quite well that it is Sunday, and wont attempt to go
with me." She was perfectly right.  Beau sat in a
chair, watching her through the open window, as she
drove off, looking the picture of mortified resignation,
but not offering to quit his place, though he had not
been told to remain there.

64. A more remarkable story has been handed down
from the last generation in our family, which, although
I cannot vouch for its authenticity, I fully believe.  In
this instance, it was a favourite Pomeranian dog, who,
having been several times prevented from following the
family to church, a distance of about a mile and a half
from the house, used to start some time before them,
and getting into their pew, remain perdu there until
they came, when it was thought better to allow him to
remain quietly where he was, than make a disturbance
by turning him out

65. A vessel was driven on the beach at Lydd, in
Kent.  The surf was rolling furiously.  Eight poor
fellows were crying for help, but no boat could be got
off to their assistance.  At length, a gentleman came on

the beach, accompanied by his Newfoundland dog. He directed the attention of the animal to the vessel, and put a short stick into his mouth. The intelligent and courageous fellow at once understood his meaning, and sprang into the sea and fought his way through the waves. He could not, however, get close enough to the vessel to deliver that with which he was charged, but the crew joyfully made fast a rope to another piece of wood, and threw it towards him. He saw the whole business in an instant; he dragged it through the surge, and delivered it to his master. A line of communication was thus formed, and every man on board was rescued from a watery grave. There is no breed to which the Newfoundland shall yield in intelligence and noble spirit, except him of Mount St. Bernard, and perhaps the Scotch colley or sheep-dog.

66. The well known dogs of the convent of Mount St. Bernard deserve more than a passing tribute. If they find a child amid the snows, they stay not for instructions, but hasten with it to the hospitable monks. Of their own accord, they roam about these desolate regions day and night, seeking to relieve the distresses of travellers. One of these dogs has a cask of cordial tied about his neck, to which the sufferer may apply for support; and another has a warm cloak about his back, to cover him. It is related that one of these indispensable animals had saved the lives of twenty-two persons, and was at last buried in an avalanche, in attempting to convey a poor courier to his family, who were toiling up the mountain to meet him : all were lost in one common calamity.

67. A gentleman was missed in London, and was supposed to have met with some foul play. No clue could be obtained to the mystery, till it was gained from observing his dog continue to crouch down before a certain house. The animal would not be induced to leave the spot, and it was at length inferred that he might be waiting for his master. The house, hitherto above suspicion, was searched, and the result was the discovery of the body of the missing individual, who had been murdered. The guilty parties were arrested, confessed their crime ; and thus one of the " dens of London" were broken up by the " police knowledge " of the faithful dog.

68. The morning service at a church not far from Gloucester, was interupted in rather a strange manner on Sunday. The incumbent happens to have an ex-ceedingly fine dog, to which he is greatly attached, and while the reverend gentlemen was preaching, his canine favourite walked into the pulpit, and quietly laid his head near the manuscript sermon. The preacher, though at first somewhat disconcerted, speedily recover-ed himself, and led the disturber out of the church, and then returned to the pulpit and resumed his discourse.

69. Here is another example of generosity. A favourite house-dog, left to the care of its master's servants at Edinburgh while he was himself in the country, would have been starved by them had it not had recourse to the kitchen of a friend of its master's which it occasionally visited. Not content with in-dulging himself simply in this freak of good fortune, this liberal-minded animal, a few days subsequently,

falling in with a poor solitary duck, and possibly deeming it to be in destitute circumstances, caught it up in his teeth, and carried it to the well-stored larder that had so amply supplied his own necessities. He laid the duck at the cook's feet, with many polite movements of his tail,— the most expressive of canine features,— then scampered off, with much seeming complacency at having given his hostess this substantial proof of his grateful sense of favours received.

70. Take another instance of canine devotion, that of a dog whose master desired him to guard a bag, which he had inadvertently placed almost in the middle of a narrow street, in the town of Southampton. While the faithful animal was keeping watch over it, a cart passed by, and such was the immovable determination of the creature to obey his master's orders, that, rather than relinquish his trust, he actually suffered the vehicle to crush him to death.

71. In 1851, a dog of the Newfoundland breed was brought to the manse of Gamrie, and being intended for a watch, was put upon chain. His food was supplied him from a wooden box, which, when fully charged, contained a more liberal allowance than was rather agreeable or convenient to discuss at a meal; and hence it happened that not unfrequently a considerable portion remained over. The discovery was soon made by certain domestics of the feathered tribe, and in endeavouring to turn it to their advantage, one, two, and three ruthlessly perished in the jaws of the proper owner. For these violent proceedings, a sound flogging was the ready punishment awarded the dog, and he

soon left off the habit; but in the peculating practices
of the feathered bipeds no improvement took place
It was too much to have, from time to time, passively
to witness this unwarrantable appropriation of his
property, and the natural means of redress man-re-
strained.   What could he do?   Retire to his couch,
there to avoid the pain of seeing what he deplored but
could not prevent.  And this was tried.   Not however,
proving satisfactory, the dog is seen emerging from his
concealment, and the next moment a sudden spring
lodges his head in the midst of the knot of larcenists,
when rout and confusion ensued.  Another one has
perished!  Nothing of the kind.  The space is only
cleared, and the box in the firm hold of Neptune's
ample jaws.   Thus having rescued his own, he bears
it in triumph to his stronghold, and stows it away in the
securest corner, that, when the calls of nature prompted,
himself only should appropriate any remainder of
provisions the vessel might contain.   Nor was the feat
left unimproved.   When the time of feeding came
round, the dish was lifted from its secrecy, and suitably
placed on the promenade, to receive, no doubt, the
expected and necessary supplies, a morsel of which
was never thereafter known to have been left exposed
to the predatory visits of unscrupulous vagrant hordes.

72. Pen being in hand, I may also transmit the
following anecdote of a dog of the English terrier kind,
which for several years was an inmate of my father's
family.   At the period referred to, the oldest member of
the family was in early childhood, and as is common in
the like circumstances, the child and the dog were

mutual favourites, and had much mutual enjoyment in
fun and frolic. A day came however, on which a sudden
snarl, expressive of temper and violence on the dog's
part, interrupted the usual cordiality of these friendly
exchanges, and the ever-watchful mother, alarmed for
the sake of her child, immediately rushed on the dog,
and violently drove him away, feeling assured he had
inflicted damage. But nothing of the sort was apparent,
not even after the minutest inspection, and the outcry
and alarm soon passed away. Meantime the dog had
not ventured from the corner of disgrace into which he
had been driven, but was observed to maintain an
attitude of regret, and only after the ado had thoroughly
subsided, and matters resumed their usual aspect, did
he begin to move. Advancing slowly towards the
amiable guardian of his accustomed playmate, and finding he was not repelled, he plants himself at last, directly
before her, and with a somewhat more than half assured
touch of his paw, solicited attention. It was given, and
forthwith something is deposited at the mother's foot.
It is a pin, the lifting and examination of which the
dog watched, with an eye we presume dogs in difficulties
can only employ. The pleading was too direct not to
be understood, for here was at once the instrument of
offence, and the element of proof, the case made his
own, and its history disclosed! The pin had come in
the child's way, and in the turns of fun, the dog's nose
was to be a pincushion. But the snarl rebuked the
offence, and the snap safely removed the dangerous and
cruel weapon from unsafe hands. Thus all became at
once right again, and the dog's first movement was back

2 F

to the child, to assure it of forgiveness, strike hands
and be friends, which they ever after were.

73. Mr. L had two dogs ;—a very large and powerful
one, called " Hero ; " a smaller, named " Tiny." The
master was sitting by the fire, half asleep, after dinner;
Hero seemed just asleep under the dining table ; Tiny
came in whining, with a terrible tale to Hero, who was
unceremoniously aroused from his slumbers to hear the
complaint of his diminutive companion, Little time
was taken to consider the course to be adopted. Both
rushed from the house ; Hero took the yard gate at a
bound, and Tiny as quickly through the spars, when a
tremendous uproar in the street soon brought the master
to the spot, where Hero had turned another very
powerful dog on his back, while Tiny was shaking the
undermost in his tenderest part.   The unfortunate
object of the joint attack was the butcher's dog, and
the knight of the cleaver was at once asked by Mr. L.
what it all meant, and was answered thus : Your little
cur came swaggering and snarling round my dog, who
at once gave him a shake up, and on the whipper-
snapper being released, he bolted home and brought
out your big dog, and you've seen the rest.

74. The Newfoundland is known to be superior to
most others in the power of swimming, for which it is
peculiarly fitted, by having the foot partly webbed.
Some years ago, a nurse was playing with a child on
the parapet of a bridge at Dublin.  With a sudden
spring, the child fell into the river  The agonised
spectators saw the waters close over the child, and
imagined that it had sunk to rise no more, when a

noble dog, seeing the catastrophe, gazed wistfully at the ripple in the stream made by the child's descent, and rushed in to its rescue. At the same instant, the poor little thing reappeared on the surface: the dog seized it, and with a firm but gentle pressure bore it to the shore without injury. Among the spectators attracted to the spot was a gentleman who appeared strongly impressed with admiration for the sagacity and promptness of the dog. On hastening to get near him, he saw, with terror, joy, and surprise, that the child was his own! Such was his sense of gratitude, that, it is said, he offered five hundred guineas for the noble animal.

75. In crossing the mountain St. Gothard, near Aviola, the Chevalier Gaspard de Brandenburg and his servant were buried in an avalanche. His dog, who escaped the heap of snow, did not quit the place when he had lost his master, which was fortunately not far from the convent. The animal howled almost incessantly, ran to the convent frequently, and alternately returned. Astonished at his repeated visits, the people of the house, on the following morning, obeyed his interceding indications, and accompanied him to the spot; where, by scratching the snow with his utmost strength and persevering zeal, they were induced to conjecture the cause; and, by speedily removing the snow, the Chevalier and his servant were recovered unhurt, after thirty-six hours confinement beneath the snow, during which they could distinctly hear the howling of the dog, and the conversation of their deliverers. Sensible, that, to the fondness and sagacity

of this creature he owed his life, the gentleman ordered,
by his will, that he should be represented on his tomb
with his dog. And at Zug, in the church of St. Oswald,
where he was buried, in 1728, they still shew the
monument, and the effigy of this gentleman, with the
dog lying at his feet.

76. On the south-west extremity of Knowle Common,
near the Great Western Station at Birmingham, is a
cottage inhabited by a labouring man named Hands.
Having but a scanty subsistence, both he and his wife
are necessarily absent from home during the greater
part of the day. The cottage is then left to the care of
four children, the eldest being but nine years of age.
This was the case on the morning of Wednesday,
when, just as the snow began falling, the youngest
child, a girl three years old, was sent to gather a few
sticks. The child did not come back, and but little
concern was felt, until the mother, unexpectedly returning home about two o'clock, was told of the
circumstance. She at once surmised some evil had
befallen the little creature; and, while looking about
in a state of frenzy, communicated her apprehensions
to a gentlemen living in the immediate neighbourhood.
Prompted by sympathy for the poor woman, but with a
very vague idea as to any assistance he could render,
he left his residence, followed by a small spaniel. He
had not proceeded far, when the dog was suddenly
missed; but, though the snow fell thickly, and evening
was fast approaching, he was enabled to track him in
the direction of a shallow well, which formerly received
the land-soak, but which an improved system of

drainage has long rendered dry and useless. For
safety, however, the mouth of the pit has been covered
over. At this spot, the dog was descried scratching
with violence, and whining most impatiently. The
gentleman now pressed forward with eagerness, thinking some game might possibly be sheltering near; but,
on arriving at the well, and lifting the lid, to his
amazement he beheld the child, whose loss had spread
anxiety throughout the neighbourhood. It was evident,
from the partial decay of the supports, that the child
must have trodden upon the insecure side of the cover,
which, yielding to her step, suffered her to fall in, and,
re adjusting itself by its own weight, closed like a trap.
The little innocent was in a standing posture, and
comparatively unhurt, but too far beneath the surface
to make a successful effort for its own deliverance.
Immediate suffocation was fortunately prevented by a
lateral opening into a neighbouring drain. Nevertheless, but for the accidental discovery, the doom of the
child was inevitable, either from starvation, or from
drowning, had a thaw ensued.

77. I one day picked up in the street an old spaniel,
which some boys were worrying, and whom natural
timidity rendered incapable of defending herself.
Grateful for the protection, she readily followed me
home, in expectation of finding an owner for her, but
which not happening, she spent the remainder of her
life, three or four years, in this asylum. Convinced
she was safe and well treated, I had few opportunities
of particularly noticing her afterwards, and she attached herself principally to the man who fed her. At a

future period, when inspecting the sick dogs, I observed
her in great pain, occasionally crying out. After some
difficulty, I relieved her by an operation; and the
relief she instantly felt produced an effect I shall
never forget. She licked my hands, and when put on
the ground she did the same to my feet, danced round
me, and screamed with gratitude and joy. From this
time to her death, which did not happen till two years
after, she never forgot the benefit she had received.
On the contrary, whenever I approached, she was
boisterous in evincing her gratitude and regard,
and would never let me rest till, by noticing her
I had convinced her that I was sensible of her
caresses. The difference between her behaviour before
this accident, and after it, was so pointed and striking,
that it was impossible to mistake the grateful sense
she had ever retained of the kindness which had been
shown to her.

78. One of the most striking instances which we
have heard, say the Messrs. Chambers, of sagacity and
personal attachment in the shepherd's dog, occurred
about half a century ago among the Grampian mountains. In one of his excursions to his distant flocks
in these high pasturages, a shepherd happened to carry
along with him one of his children, an infant about
three years old. After traversing this pasture for some
time, attended by his dog, the shepherd found himself
under the necessity of ascending a summit at some
distance, to have a more extensive view of his range.
As the ascent was too fatiguing for the child, he left
him on a small plain at the bottom, with strict injunc-

tions not to stir from it till his return. Scarcely, however, had he gained the summit, when the horizon was suddenly darkened by one of those impenetrable mists which frequently descend so rapidly amidst these mountains, as, in the space of a few minutes, almost to turn day into night. The anxious father instantly hastened back to find his child; but, owing to the unusual darkness, and his own trepidation, he unfortunately missed his way in the descent. After a fruitless search of many hours amongst the dangerous morasses and cataracts with which these mountains abound, he was at length overtaken by night. Still wandering on without knowing whither, he at length came to the verge of the mist, and, by the light of the moon, discovered that he had reached the bottom of the valley, and was within a short distance of his cottage. To renew the search that night was equally fruitless and dangerous. He was therefore obliged to return to his cottage, having lost both his child and his dog, which had attended him faithfully for years. Next morning, by day-break, the shepherd, accompanied by a band of his neighbours, set out in search of his child; but, after a day spent in fruitless fatigue, he was at last compelled, by the approach of night, to descend from the mountain. On returning to his cottage, he found that the dog, which he had lost the day before, had been home, and, on receiving a piece of cake, had instantly gone off again. For several successive days the shepherd renewed the search for his child, and still, on returning at evening disappointed to his cottage, he found that the dog had been home, and, on receiving his usual allowance of cake, had instantly disappeared. Struck with this singular circumstance, he remained at home one day, and when the dog as usual departed with his piece of cake, he resolved to follow him, and find out the cause of his strange procedure. The dog led the way to a cataract, at some distance from the spot where the shepherd had left his child. The banks of the cataract almost joined at the top, yet, separated by an abyss of immense depth, presented that appearance which so often astonishes and appals the travellers who frequent the Grampian mountains, and indicates that these stupendous chasms were not the silent work of time, but the sudden effect of some violent convulsion of the earth. Down one of these rugged and almost perpendicular descents the dog began, without hesitation, to make his way, and at last disappeared into a cave, the mouth of which was almost upon a level with the torrent. The shepherd with difficulty followed; but, on entering the cave, what were his emotions when he beheld his infant eating with much satisfaction the cake which the dog had just brought him, while the faithful animal stood by, eyeing his young charge with the utmost complacence. From the situation in which the child was found, it appears that he had wandered to the brink of the precipice, and then either fallen or scrambled down, till he reached the cave, which the dread of the torrent had afterwards prevented him from quitting. The dog, by means of his scent, had traced him to the spot; and afterwards prevented him from starving, by giving up to him his own daily allowance. He appears never to have quitted the child by night or day, except when it was necessary to go for his food, and then he was always seen running at full speed to and from the cottage.

79. The benevolence of dogs generally, but the Newfoundland variety in particular, has often excited marks of high admiration. A writer on this subject observes that he once saw a water-spaniel, unbidden, plunge into the current of a roaring sluice to save a small cur, maliciously thrown in.

80. The same motive seemed to animate a Pomeranian dog, belonging to a Dutch vessel. This creature sprang overboard, caught a child up, and swam on shore with it, before any person had discovered the accident.

81. A child, playing on Roshe's Wharf with a Newfoundland dog belonging to his father, accidentally fell into the water. The dog immediately sprang after the child, who was only six years old, and seizing the waist of his little frock, brought him into the dock, where there was a stage, by which the child held on, but was unable to get on the top. The dog, seeing it was unable to pull the little fellow out of the water, ran up to the yard adjoining, where a girl, of nine years of age, was hanging out clothes. He seized the girl by the frock, and notwithstanding her exertions to get away, he succeeded in dragging her to the spot where the child was still hanging by the hands to the stage. On the girl's taking hold of the child, the dog assisted her in rescuing the little fellow from his perilous situation, and after licking the face of the infant it had thus saved, it took a leap off the stage, and swam

round to the end of the wharf, and immediately after
returned with his hat in his mouth.

82. The most remarkable anecdote of this class,
however, is that regarding a Swiss chamois-hunter's
dog. This animal being on the glaciers with an English
gentleman and his master, observed the first approaching one of those awful crevices in the ice to look down
into it. He began to slide towards the edge ; his guide,
with a view to save him, caught his coat, and both slid
onward, till the dog seized his master's clothes, and
arrested them both from inevitable death. The gentleman left the dog a pension for life.

83. Very extraordinary stories have been told of dogs
discovering and circumventing plans to injure the
persons of their masters, in which it is difficult to place
implicit credit. We give one of the most marvellous of
these anecdotes, as it is usually related. Sir H. Lee, of
Ditchley, in Oxfordshire, ancestor of the Earls of Lich-
field, had a mastiff which guarded the house and yard,
but had never met with any particular attention from
his master. In short, he was not a favourite dog, and
was retained for his utility only, and not from any
partial regard. One night, as Sir Harry was retiring to
his chamber, attended by his favourite valet, an Italian,
the mastiff silently followed them up stairs, which he
had never been known to do before, and, to his master's
astonishment, presented himself in the bed room.
Being deemed an intruder, he was instantly ordered to
be turned out, which, being complied with, the poor
animal began scratching violently at the door, and
howling loudly for admission. The servant was sent

to drive him away. Discouragement, however, could not check his intended labour of love; he returned again, and was more importunate to be let in than before. Sir Harry, weary of opposition, though surprised beyond measure at the dog's apparent fondness for the society of his master who had never shown him the least kindness, and wishing to retire to rest, bade the servant open the door that they might see what he wanted to do. This done, the mastiff, with a wag of the tail, and a look of affection at his lord, deliberately walked up, and crawling under the bed, laid himself down, as if desirous to take up his night's lodgings there. To save farther trouble, and not from any partiality for his company, this indulgence was allowed. The valet withdrew, and all was still. About the solemn hour of midnight the chamber door opened, and a person was heard stepping across the room. Sir Harry started from sleep; the dog sprang from his covert, and seizing the unwelcome disturber, fixed him to the spot. All was dark: Sir Harry rang his bell in great trepidation, in order to procure a light. The person who was pinned to the floor by the courageous mastiff roared for assistance. It was found to be the favourite valet, who little expected such a reception. He endeavoured to apologise for his intrusion, and to make the reasons which induced him to take this step appear plausible; but the importunity of the dog, the time, the place, the manner of the valet, raised suspicions in Sir Harry's mind, and he determined to refer the investigation of the business to a magistrate. The perfidious Italian, alternately terrified by the dread of punishment,

and soothed by the hope of pardon, at length confessed
that it was his intention to murder his master, and then
rob the house. This diabolical design was frustrated
solely by the unaccountable sagacity of the dog, and
devoted atachment to his master. A full-length picture
of Sir Harry, with the mastiff by his side, and the
words, " More faithful than favoured," is still preserved
among the family pictures.

84. The presentiment of approaching danger, of which
we have given the above example, evinces a higher
degree of reasoning power than that shown in ordinary
acts of sagacity or personal attachment. In the notice
given by Captain Fitzroy of the earthquake at Galca-
huasco, on the 20th of February 1835, it is mentioned
that all the dogs had left the town before the great
shock which ruined the buildings was felt.

85. A French author has related an amusing instance
of canine independence. He states that, at the beginning of the Revolution, there was a dog in Paris known
by the name of Parade, because he always attended
regularly the military parades at the Tuileries. A taste
for music was probably the cause of this fancy. He
always stood by, and marched with the band, and at
night went to the Opera, Comedic Italiene, or Theatre
Feydau, dined with any musician who expressed, by
word or gesture, that his company was asked, yet always
withdrew from attempts to be made the property of
any individual.

86. The educability of the dog's perceptive faculties
has been exemplified in a remarkable manner by his
acquired knowledge of musical sounds. On some dogs

fine music produces an apparently painful effect, causing them gradually to become restless, to moan piteously, and, finally, to fly from the spot with every sign of suffering and distress. Others have been seen to sit and listen to music with seeming delight, and even to go every Sunday to church, with the obvious purpose of enjoying the solemn and powerful strains of the organ. Some dogs manifest a keen sense of false notes in music. Our friend Mrs. S. C. Hall, at Old Brompton, say the Messrs. Chambers of Edinburgh, possesses an Italian greyhound which screams in apparent agony when a jarring combination of notes is produced accidentally or intentionally on the piano. These opposite and various manifestations show what might be done by education to teach dogs a critical knowledge of sounds.

87. A gentleman of Darmstadt, in Germany, as we learn, has taught a poodle dog to detect false notes in music. We give the account of this remarkable instance of educability as it appears in a French newspaper. Mr. S———, having acquired a competency by commercial industry, retired from business, and devoted himself, heart and soul, to the cultivation and enjoyment of music. Every member of his little household was by degrees involved more or less in the same occupation, and even the housemaid could in time bear a part in a chorus, or decipher a melody of Schubert. One individual alone in the family seemed to resist this musical entrancement ; this was a small spaniel, the sole specimen of the canine race in the mansion. Mr. S——— felt the imposibility of instilling the theory

G

of sounds into the head of Poodle, but he firmly resolved to make the animal bear *some* part or other in
the general domestic concert; and by perseverence,
and the adoption of ingenious means, he attained his
object.   Every time that a *false note* escaped either
from instrument or voice—as often as any blunder,
of whatever kind, was committed by the members of
the musical family (and such blunders were sometimes
committed intentionally)—down came its master's cane
on the back of the unfortunate Poodle, till she howled
and growled again.   Poodle perceived the meaning of
these unkind chastisements, and instead of becoming
sulky, showed every disposition to howl on the instant
a false note was uttered, without waiting for the form-
ality of a blow.   By and by, a mere glance of Mr. S——'s
eye was sufficient to make the animal howl to admiration.    In the end, Poodle became so thoroughly
acquainted with, and attentive to, false notes and other
musical barbarisms, that the slightest mistake of the kind
was infallibly signalised by a yell from her, forming the
most expressive commentary upon the misperformance.
When extended trials were made of the animal's
acquirements, they were never found to fail, and Poodle
became, what she still is, the most famous, impartial,
and conscientious connoisseur in the duchy of Hesse.
But, as may be imagined, her musical appreciation is
entirely negative; if you sing with expression, and
play with ability, she will remain cold and impassable.
But let your execution exhibit the slightest defect, and
you will have her instantly showing her teeth, whisking
her tail, yelping, barking and growling.   At the present

time, there is not a concert or an opera at Darmstadt to which Mr. S—— and his wonderful dog are not invited, or, at least, *the dog*. The voice of the prima donna, the instruments of the band—whether violin, clarionet, hautbois, or bugle—all of them must execute their parts in perfect harmony, otherwise Poodle looks at its master, erects its ears, shows its grinders, and howls outright. Old or new pieces, known or unknown to the dog, produce on it the same effect. It must not be supposed that the discrimination of the creature is confined to the mere *execution* of musical compositions. Whatever must have been the case at the outset of its training, its present and perfected intelligence extends even to the secrets of composition. Thus, if a vicious modulation, or a false relation of parts, occurs in a piece of music, the animal shows symptoms of uneasy hesitation, and if the error be continued, will infallibly give the grand condemnatory howl. In short, Poodle is the terror of all middling composers of Darmstadt, and a perfect nightmare to the imagination of all poor singers and players. Sometimes Mr. S—— and his friends take a pleasure in annoying the canine critic, by emitting all sorts of discordant sounds from instrument and voice. On such occasions the creature loses all self-command, its eyes shoot forth fiery flashes, and long and frightful howls respond to the immelodious concert of mischievous bipeds. But the latter must be careful not to go too far; for when the dog's patience is tried to excess, it becomes altogether wild, and flies fiercely at the tormentors and their instruments. This dog's case is a very curious one, and the attendant phenomena not very easy of explanation. From the animal's power of discriminating the correctness of musical composition, as well as of execution, one would be inclined to imagine that Mr. S——, in training his dog, had only called into play faculties existing (but latent) before, and that dogs have in them the natural germs of a fine musical ear. This seems more likely to be the case, than that the animal's perfect musical taste was wholly an acquirement, resulting from the training. However this may be, the Darmstadt dog is certainly a marvellous creature, and we are surprised that, in these exhibiting times, its powers have not been displayed on a wider stage. The operatic establishments of London and Paris might be greatly the better, perhaps, of a visit from the critical Poodle.

88. It is now settled, as a philosophical question, remark the Messrs. Chambers, that the instruction communicated to dogs, as well as various other animals, has a hereditary effect on the progeny. If a dog be taught to perform certain feats, the young of the dog will be much easier initiated in the same feats than other dogs. Thus, the existing races of English pointers are greatly more accomplished in their required duties than the original race of Spanish spaniels. Dogs of the St. Bernard variety inherit the faculty of tracking footsteps in the snow. A gentleman of our acquaintance, and of scientific acquirements, obtained, some years ago, a pup which had been produced in London by a female of the celebrated St. Bernard breed. The young animal was brought to Scotland, where it was never observed to give any particular

tokens of a power of tracking footsteps until winter, when the ground became covered with snow. It *then* showed the most active inclination to follow footsteps; and so great was its power of doing so under these circumstances, that, when its master had crossed a field in the most curvilinear way, and caused other persons to cross his path in all directions, it nevertheless followed his course with the greatest precision. Here was a perfect revival of the habit of its Alpine fathers, with a degree of speciality as to external conditions, at which, it seems to us, we cannot sufficiently wonder.

89. About sixty years ago, the Messrs. Chambers relate, a Frenchman brought to London from eighty to a hundred dogs, chiefly poodles, the remainder spaniels, but all nearly of the same size, and of the smaller kind. On the education of these animals, their proprietor had bestowed an immense deal of pains. From puppyhood upwards, they had been taught to walk on their hind legs, and maintain their footing with surprising ease in that unnatural position. They had likewise been drilled into the best possible behaviour towards each other; no snarling, barking, or indecorous conduct took place when they were assembled in company. But what was most surprising of all, they were able to perform in various theatrical pieces, of the character of pantomimes, representing various transactions in heroic and familiar life, with wonderful fidelity. The object of their proprietor was, of course, to make money by their performances, which the public were accordingly invited to witness in one of the minor theatres. Amongst their histrionic performances was

2 G

the representation of a siege. On the rising of the
curtain, there appeared three ranges of ramparts, one
above the other, having salient angles, and a moat, like
a regularly constructed fortification. In the centre of
the fortress arose a tower, on which a flag was flying;
while, in the distance behind, appeared the buildings
and steeples of a town. The ramparts were guarded
by soldiers in uniform, each armed with a musket or
sword, of an appropriate size. All these were dogs,
and their duty was to defend the walls from an attacking party, consisting also of dogs, whose movements
now commenced the operations of the siege. In the
foreground of the stage were some rude buildings and
irregular surfaces, from among which there issued a
reconnoitring party; the chief, habited as an officer of
rank, with great circumspection surveyed the fortification, and his sedate movements, and his consultations
with the troops that accompanied him, implied that an
attack was determined upon. But these consultations
did not pass unobserved by the defenders of the
garrison. The party was noticed by a sentinel, and
fired upon, and this seemed to be the signal to call
every man to his post at the embrasures. Shortly
after, the troops advanced to the escalade; but to cross
the moat, and get at the bottom of the walls, it was
necessary to bring up some species of pontoon, and,
accordingly, several soldiers were seen engaged in
pushing before them wicker-work scaffoldings, which
moved on castors, towards the fortifications. The
drums beat to arms, and the fearful bustle of warfare
opened in earnest. Smoke was poured out in volleys

from shot-holes; the besieging forces pushed forward
in masses, regardless of the fire; the moat was filled
with the crowd; and, amid much confusion and scrambling, scaling-ladders were raised against the walls.
Then was the grand tug of war. The leaders of the
forlorn hope who first ascended, were opposed with
great gallantry by the defenders; and this was perhaps
the most interesting part of the exhibition. The chief
of the assailants did wonders: he was seen now here,
now there, animating his men, and was twice hurled,
with ladder and followers, from the second gradation
of ramparts; but he was invulnerable, and seemed to
receive an accession of courage on every fresh repulse.
The scene became of an exciting nature. The rattle of
the miniature cannon, the roll of the drums, the sound
of trumpets, and the heroism of the actors on both
sides, imparted an idea of reality, that, for the moment,
made the spectator forget that he was looking on a
performance of dogs. Not a bark was heard in the
struggle. After numerous hair-breadth escapes, the
chief surmounted the third line of fortifications, followed by his troops; the enemy's standard was hurled
down, and the British flag hoisted in its place; the
ramparts were manned by the conquerors; and the
smoke cleared away—to the tune of "God save the
King." It is impossible to convey a just idea of this
performance, which altogether reflected great credit
on its contriver, as also on the abilities of each individual dog. We must conclude that the firing from
the embrasures and some other parts of the mechanique
were effected by human agency, but the actions of the

dogs were clearly their own, and showed what could
be effected with animals by dint of patient culture.
90. Another specimen of these canine theatricals was
quite a contrast to the bustle of the siege. The scene
was an assembly-room, on the sides and the farther
end of which seats were placed, while a music-gallery
and a profusion of chandeliers gave a richness and
truth to the general effect. Livery-servants were in
attendance on a few of the company, who entered and
took their seats. Frequent knockings now occurred at
the door, followed by the entrance of parties attired in
the fashion of the period. These were, of course, the
same individuals who had recently been in the deadly
breach; but now all was tranquillity, elegance, and
ease. Parties were formally introduced to each other,
with an appearance of the greatest decorum, though
sometimes a young dog would shew a slight disposition
to break through restraint, but only to the increased
amusement of the beholders. Some of the dogs that
represented ladies were dressed in silks, gauzes, laces,
and gay tasteful ribbons. Some wore artificial flowers,
with the flowing ringlets of youth; others wore the
powdered and pomatumed head-dress of riper years,
with caps and lappets, in ludicrous contrast to the
features of the animals. Doubtless the whole had
been the result of judicious study and correct arrangement, for the most animated were habited as the most
youthful. The animals which represented gentlemen
were judiciously equipped; some as youthful, and
others as aged beaux, regulated by their degrees of
proficiency, since those most youthfully dressed were

most attentive to the ladies. The frequent bow, and return of curtsey, produced great mirth in the audience; but when the noses of the animals neared each other, it produced a shriek of delight from the youthful spectators. On a sudden the master of the ceremonies appeared. No doubt he was the chief in the battle fray. He was now an elegant fellow, full of animation; he wore a superb court-dress, and his manners were in agreement with his costume. He approached many of the visitors : to some of the gentlemen he gave merely a look of recognition; to the ladies he was generally attentive; to some he projected his paw familiarly, to others he bowed with respect, and introduced one to another with an air of elegance that surprised and delighted the spectators. There was a general feeling of astonishment at some of the nicer features of the scene, as at the various degrees of intimacy which individuals expressed by their nods and bows of recognition. As the performance advanced, the interest increased. A little music was heard as from the gallery, but it was soon interrupted by a loud knocking, which announced the arrival of some important visitor, and expectation was raised. Several livery servants entered, and then a sedan-chair was borne in by appropriately dressed dogs; they removed the poles, raised the head, and opened the door of the sedan; forth came a lady, splendidly attired in spangled satin and jewels, and her head decorated with a plume of ostrich feathers! She made a great impression, and appeared as if conscious of her superior attraction. Meanwhile the chair was removed, the master of the ceremonics, in his court-dress, was in readiness to receive the *élégante,* the bow and curtsey were admirably interchanged, and an air of elegance pervaded the deportment of both. The band now struck up an air of the kind to which ball-room companies are accustomed to promenade, and the company immediately quitted their seats, and began to walk ceremoniously in pairs round the room. Three of the ladies placed their arms under those of their attendant gentlemen. On seats being resumed, the master of the ceremonies and the lady who came in the sedan-chair arose; he led her to the centre of the room; Foote's minuet struck up; the pair commenced the movements with an attention to time; they performed the crossings and turnings, the advancings, retreatings, and obeisances, during which there was a perfect silence; and they concluded amid thunders of applause. What ultimately became of the ingenious manager with his company, our informant never heard.

91. Perhaps the most remarkable instance known of what are called "learned dogs" is that of two poodles, which were trained at Milan, and exhibited at Paris in the spring of 1830. The account of them is given by a lady whose veracity is not doubtful, and who herself saw their performance. The elder named Fido, says she, is white, with some black patches on his head and back; and the younger who is called Bianco, is also white but with red spots. Fido is a grave and serious personage, walks with dignity round the circle assembled to see him, and appears much absorbed in reflection. Bianco is young and giddy, but full of talent

when he chooses to apply it. Owing to his more sedate
disposition, however, Fido is called upon to act the
principal part of the exhibition. A word is dictated to
him from the Greek, Latin, Italian, German, French,
or English language, and selected from a vocabulary
where fifty words in such tongue are inscribed, and
which altogether make three hundred different com-
binations. An alphabet is placed before Fido, and
from it he takes the letters which compose the given
word, and lays them in proper order at the feet of his
master. On one occasion he was told to spell the word
heathen, and he quickly placed the letters till he came
to the second e; he stood for an instant as if puzzled,
but in a moment after he took the e out of the first
syllable, and put it into the second. His attainments
in orthography, however, are not so surprising as those
in arithmetic. He practises the four rules with extraordinary facility, arranges the double ciphers as he did
in the word heathen, and rarely makes an error. When
such does occur, his more thoughtless companion is
called to rectify it, which he invariably does with the
greatest quickness ; but as he had rather play than
work, and pulls Fido by the ears to make him as idle
as himself, he is quickly dismissed. One day, the
steady Fido spelt the word Jupiter with a b instead of
a p ; Bianco was summoned to his aid, who, after con-
templating the word, pushed out the b with his nose,
and seizing a p between his teeth put it into the va-
cancy. Fido is remarkable for the modest firmness
with which he insists upon his correctness when he
feels convinced of it himself, for a lady having struck

a repeating watch in his ear, he selected an 8 for the
hour, and a 6 for the three quarters. The company
present, and his master, called out to him he was
wrong. He reviewed his numbers and stood still. His
master insisted, and he again examined his ciphers;
after which he went quietly, but not in the least abash-
ed, into the middle of the carpet, and looked at his
audience. The watch was then sounded again, and it
was found to have struck two at every quarter, and
Fido received the plaudits which followed with as gentle a demeanour as that with which he had borne the
accusation of error. One occupation seems to bring
the giddy Bianco to the gravity of the elder savan, and
when the spectators are tired of arithmetic and orthography, the two dogs either sit down to écarté, or
become the antagonists of one of the company. They
ask for, or refuse cards, as their hands require, with a
most important look; they cut at the proper times,
and never mistake one suit for another. They have
recourse to their ciphers to mark their points; and, on
one occasion, Bianco having won, he selected his number, and on being asked what were the gains of his
adversary, he immediately took an 0 between his teeth,
and showed it to the querist, and both seemed to
know all the terms of the game as thoroughly as the
most experienced card-players. All this passes without
the slightest visible or audible sign between the
poodles and master. The spectators are placed within
three steps of the carpet on which the performance
goes forward; people have gone for the sole purpose of
watching the master; every body visits them, and yet

no one has hitherto found out the mode of communication established between them and their owner.
Whatever this communication may be, it does not
deduct from the wonderful intelligence of these animals; for there must be a multiplicity of signs, not
only to be understood with eyes and ears, but to be
separated from each other in their minds, or to be combined one with another, for the various trials in which
they are exercised. I have seen learned pigs and
ponies, and can, after these spectacles, readily imagine
how the extraordinary sagacity of a dog may be brought
to a knowledge of the orthography of three hundred
words. But I must confess myself puzzled by the *
acquirements of these poodles in arithmetic, which
must depend upon the will of the spectator who pro-
poses the numbers. But that which is most surprising
of all is the skill with which they play *écarté*. The
gravity and attention with which they carry on their
game, is almost ludicrous; and the satisfaction of
Bianco when he marks his points is perfectly evident.

92. Fully as interesting an exhibition of clever dogs
took place in London in the summer of 1843, under
the auspices of M. Leonard, a French gentleman of
scientific attainments and enlightened character, who
had for some years directed his attention to the reasoning powers of animals, and their cultivation. Two
pointers, Braque and Philax, had' been the especial
objects of his instruction, and their naturally inferior
intellectual capacities had been excited in an extraordinary degree. A writer in the Atlas newspaper
thus speaks of the exhibition of these animals :— " M.

Leonard's dogs are not merely clever, well taught animals, which, by dint of practice, can pick up a particular letter, or can, by a sort of instinct, indicate a number which may be asked for; they call into action, powers which, if not strictly intellectual, approx imate very closely to reason. For instance, they exert memory. Four pieces of paper were placed upon the floor, which the company numbered indiscriminately, 2, 4, 6, 8. The numbers were named but once, and yet the dogs were able to pick up any one of them at command, although they were not placed in regular order. The numbers were then changed, with a similar result. Again: different objects were placed upon the floor, and when a similar thing—say a glove—was exhibited, one or other of the animals picked it up immediately. The dogs distinguish colours, and, in short, appear to understand everything that is said to them. The dog Braque plays a game of dominoes with any one who likes. We are aware that this has been done before; but when it is considered that it is necessary to distinguish the number of spots, it must be admitted that this requires the exercise of a power little inferior to reason. The dog sits on the chair with the dominoes before him; and when his adversary plays, he scans each of his dominoes with an air of attention and gravity which is perfectly marvellous. When he could not match the dominoe played, he became restless, and shook his head, and gave other indications of his inability to do so. No human being could have paid more attention. The dog seemed to watch the game with deep interest, and what is more, he won. Another point strongly indicative of the close approach to the reasoning powers, was the exactness with which the dogs obeyed an understood signal. It was agreed that when three blows were struck upon a chair, Philax should do what was requested; and when five were given, that the task should devolve on Braque. This arrangement was strictly adhered to. We do not intend to follow the various proofs which were afforded of the intelligence of the dogs; it is sufficient to say that a multiplicity of directions given to them were obeyed implicitly, and that they appeared to understand what their master said as well as any individual in the room. M. Leonard entered into a highly interesting explanation of his theory regarding the intellectual powers of animals, and the mode he adopts to train and subdue horses, exhibiting the defects of the system generally pursued. His principle is, that horses are not vicious by nature, but because they have been badly taught; and that, as with children, these defects may be corrected by proper teaching. M. Leonard does not enter into these inquiries for profit, but solely with a scientific and humane view, being desirous of investigating the extent of the reasoning powers of animals."

93. James Hogg, who possessed the best opportunities of studying the character of the shepherd's dog, mentions that he at one time had a dog, called Sirrah, an animal of sullen disposition, and by no means favourable appearance, which was an extraordinary adept in managing a flock. One of his exploits was as follows;—About seven hundred lambs, which

were once under his care at weaning-time, broke up at
midnight, and scampered off in three divisions across
the hills, in spite of all that the Shepherd and an
assistant lad could do to keep them together. ' Sirrah,'
cried the Shepherd in great affliction, ' my man, they're
a' awa.' The night was so dark, that he did not see
Sirrah ; but the faithful animal had heard his master's
words—words such as of all others were sure to set him
most on the alert; and without more ado, he silently
set off in quest of the recreant flock. Meanwhile the
Shepherd and his companion did not fail to do all that
was in their own power to recover their lost charge ;
they spent the whole night in scouring the hills for
miles around; but of neither the lambs nor Sirrah could
they obtain the slightest trace. ' It was the most extraordinary circumstance,' says the Shepherd, ' that had
ever occurred in the annals of the pastoral life. We
had nothing for it (day having dawned) but to return
to our master, and inform him that we had lost his
whole flock of lambs, and knew not what was become
of one of them. On our way home, however, we discovered a body of lambs at the bottom of a deep ravine,
called the Flech Cleuch, and the indefatigable Sirrah
standing in front of them, looking all around for some
relief, but still standing true to his charge. The
sun was then up, and when we first came in view of
them, we concluded that it was one of the divisions of
the lambs which Sirrah had been unable to manage,
until he came to that commanding situation. But what
was our astonishment when we discovered by degrees
that not one lamb of the whole flock was wanting !

How he had got all the divisions collected in the dark, is beyond my comprehension. , The charge was left entirely to himself from midnight until the rising of the sun, and if all the shepherds in the forest had been there to have assisted him, they could not have effected it with greater propriety. All that I can further say is, that I never felt so grateful to any creature below the sun, as I did to my honest Sirrah that morning.'

94. Among the narratives which still entertain the fireside circle in Tweeddale, one of the most remarkable refers to an extraordinary case of sheep-stealing, in which a shepherd's dog was a subordinate though most active agent. The case occurred in the year 1772. A young farmer in the neighbourhood of Innerleithen, whose circumstances were supposed to be good, and who was connected with many of the best storefarming families in the county, had been tempted to commit some extensive depredations upon the flocks of his neighbours, in which he was assisted by his shepherd. The pastoral farms of Tweeddale, which generally consist each of a certain range of hilly ground, had in those days no enclosures: their boundaries were indicated only by the natural features of the country. The sheep were, accordingly, liable to wander, and to become intermixed with each other, and at every reckoning of a flock, a certain allowance had been made for this, as for other contingencies. For some time Mr. William Gibson, tenant in Newby, an extensive farm stretching from the neighbourhood of Peebles to the borders of Selkirkshire, had remarked a surprising increase in the amount of his annual losses. He questioned his shep-

H

herds severely, taxed them with carelessness in picking up and bringing home the dead, and plainly intimated that he conceived some unfair dealing to be in progress. The men, finding themselves thus exposed to suspicions of a very painful kind, were as much chagrined as the worthy farmer himself, and kept their minds alive to every circumstance which might tend to afford any elucidation of the mystery. One day, while they were summering their lambs, the eye of a very acute old shepherd named Hyslop was caught by a black-faced ewe which they had formerly missed (for the shepherds generally knew every particular member of their flocks,) and which was now suckling its own lamb as if it had never been absent. On inspecting it carefully, it was found to bear an additional *birn* upon its face. Every farmer, it must be mentioned, impresses with a hot iron a particular letter upon the faces of his sheep, as a means of distinguishing his own from those of his neighbours. Mr. Gibson's brand was the letter T, and this was found distinctly enough impressed on the face of the ewe. But above this mark there was an O, which was known to be the mark of the tenant of Wormiston, the individual already mentioned. It was immediately suspected that this and the other missing sheep had been abstracted by that person; a suspicion which derived strength from the reports of the neighbouring shepherds, by whom, it appeared, the black-faced ewe had been tracked for a considerable way in a direction leading from Wormiston to Newby. It was indeed ascertained that instinctive affection for her lamb had led this animal across the Tweed, and over the lofty

heights between Cailzie and Newby, a route of very
considerable difficulty, and probably quite different
from that by which she had been led away, but the
*most direct* that could have been taken. Mr. Gibson
only stopped to obtain the concurrence of a neighbouring farmer, whose losses had been equally great, before
proceeding with' some of the legal authorities to Wormiston, where Millar, the shepherd, and his master,
were taken into custody, and conducted to the prison
of Peebles. On a search of the farm, no fewer than
thirty-three score of sheep belonging to various individuals were found, all bearing the condemnatory O
above the original *birns;* and it was remarked that
there was not a single ewe returned to Grieston, the
farm on the opposite bank of the Tweed, which did not
*minny* her lambs—that is, assume the character of
mother towards the offspring from which she had been
separated. The magnitude of this crime, the rareness
of such offences in the district, and the station in life
of at least one of the offenders, produced a great
sensation in Tweeddale, and caused the elicitation of
every minute circumstance that could possible be discovered respecting the means which had been employed
for carrying on such an extensive system of depredation.
The most surprising part of the tale is, the extent to
which it appears that the instinct of dumb animals had
been instrumental both in the crime and in its detection.
While the farmer seemed to have deputed the business
chiefly to his shepherd, the shepherd seemed to have
deputed it again, in many instances, to a dog of extraordinary sagacity, which served him in his customary

and lawful business. This animal, which bore the name of *Yarrow*, would not only act under his immediate direction in cutting off a portion of a flock, and bringing it home to Wormiston, but is said to have been able to proceed solitarily, and by night, to a sheep-walk, and there detach certain individuals previously pointed out by its master, which it would drive home by secret ways, without allowing one to straggle. It is mentioned that, while returning home with their stolen droves, they avoided, even in the night, the roads along the banks of the river, or those that descended to the valley through the adjoining glens. They chose rather to come along the ridge of mountains that separate the small river Leithen from the Tweed. But even here there was sometimes danger; for the shepherds occasionally visit their flocks before day; and often when Millar had driven his prey from a distance, and while he was yet miles from home, and the weather-gleam of the eastern hills began to be tinged with the brightening dawn, he has left them to the charge of his dog, and descended himself to the banks of the Leithen, off his way, that he might not be seen connected with their company. Yarrow, although between three and four miles from his master, would continue, with care and silence, to bring the sheep onward to Wormiston, where his master's appearance could be neither a matter of question or surprise. Near to the thatched farm-house was one of those old square towers, or peel-houses, whose picturesque ruins were then seen ornamenting the course of the Tweed, as they had been placed alternately along the north and south bank, generally from three to six hundred yard from it—sometimes on the shin, and sometimes in the hollow of a hill. In the vault of this tower it was the practice of these men to conceal the sheep they had recently stolen ; and while the rest of their people were absent on Sunday at the church, they used to employ themselves in cancelling with their knives the ear-marks, and impressing with a hot iron a large O upon the face, that covered both sides of the animal's nose, for the purpose of obliterating the brand of the true owner. While his accomplices were so busied, Yarrow kept watch in the open air, and gave notice, without fail, by his barking, of the approach of strangers. The farmer and his servant were tried at Edinburgh in January 1773, and the proceedings excited an extraordinary interest, not only in the audience, but amongst the legal officials. Hyslop the principal witness, gave so many curious particulars respecting the instincts of sheep, and the modes of distinguishing them both by natural and artificial marks, that he was highly complimented by the bench. The evidence was so complete, that both culprits were found guilty, and according to the barbarous policy of those times, they expiated their crime on the scaffold.

95. The sagacity of these interesting animals comes so very near reason in some instances, as to make it a most difficult question where instinct ends, and the rational powers begin; in other words, whether what we call reason is the exclusive property of the human creature. I remember a most singular case of intelligence in a beautiful King Charles' spaniel which belonged to my sister, which occurred a few years

since. This little animal was not only the most beautiful, but also the most touchy fellow I ever saw; but I am bound to speak well of him, because, for some reason or other, I was an especial favourite; and, although he sometimes snapped even at me, he never did more, which few others could say; and I own, although I saw his faults, I was exceedingly attached to him, and he in return had the most perfect confidence in me, and understood my looks in a most extraordinary manner; and it was a common practice, not only with myself, but other members of our family, when we left the room where he was, to promise in words to return, and not to go out without him, for his sporting propensities were very strong, and I never knew a more indefatigable, or better finder than he was. One fine day, I was engaged in my own room writing, and little "Charlie" lay on the rug dosing, and very snug and comfortable, and twice or thrice during the morning I had occasion to take my cap and go out for a few minutes, but on each occasion, promising to return, he only looked up, and again settled himself to sleep. But at last, thinking I would take a short walk, but not particularly wishing to have the encumbrance of a dog with me, I took my cap once more, and promised to return as usual; but as I passed the corner of my room, took up a small stick, which was usually my walking companion. This circumstance was sufficient to make him disbelieve what was certainly intended to deceive, and it would not accordingly do this time, for he immediately followed me to the door, showing that he was not to be done; and I own that

my heart smote me, and I took him with me, being no
less pleased with his intelligence. Now, we know, that
it is a very common thing for a dog, if you do not wish ·
him to follow you, and therefore shut him in by a front
door, to come out and join you by the back door if it
be open; or, if conscious of doing that for which he
has been chastised, on the approach of any person
immediately to decamp. But, it appears to me, that the
anecdote I have just related, is a greater refinement of
instinct than I ever heard of, or met with, and worthy
to be recorded, of a little animal who has long since
met the melancholy end of all pets; the unnatural life
he led producing asthma, which rendered it necessary
to put him into the hands of a dog doctor, where he
soon after breathed his last, and lies buried under a
small stone, in those very shrubberies which had so
often resounded to his joyous cries.

96. I well remember when a boy, at Barton-upon-
Humber, a certain "keel" employed in the Yorkshire
corn trade, on board which the captain had a dog,
possessed of some traces of terrier blood, smooth
coated, and of a pure white colour, his neck and back
adorned with stumpy bristles, which ruffled up at the
slightest provocation. Altogether, he was a mongrel
cur enough; but he was an excellent sailor, for he
attended his master on all his trading expeditions, and
never deserted his ship. One day, while the keel lay
in Barton haven, the dog was lost, and great was the
consternation in consequence. Diligent search was
made in the town and neighbourhood, but every effort
to discover the missing animal proved unavailing.

Month after month passed away, the keel went and
came on her accustomed avocations, and poor Keeper
was forgotten—considered by his master to be dead.
Judge, therefore, the man's surprise, when one day
steering with difficulty his vessel into Goole harbour,
which was crowded with shipping at the time, his
glance suddenly fell upon his faithful and long lost
dog, buffetting the water at a considerable distance
from the keel, but making eagerly towards her. By
the aid of a piece of tar rope which was dangling
round the dog's neck, and a friendly boat hook, he
was lifted, quite exhausted, on to the deck of his
master's craft, when it became at once apparent that
he had long been kept a prisoner, most probably on
board a vessel, by some one who had stolen him at
Barton.    The cause of the poor dog's sudden re-
appearance, was, undoubtedly, his having heard his
master's well remembered voice ; but it is strange he
should have been able to distinguish at so great a
distance, and when swelling that chorus of hoarse
bawlings which arises from a hundred husky throats
when a Yorkshire keel-man is engaged forcing his
craft into a crowded harbour; and it is also equally
touching, that, when roused by the distant sound, the
poor beast should have plunged, encumbered as he
was with the rope he had just burst asunder, so
gallantly into the water, an element he was ill-adapted
to move in, and in which his master declared he had
never seen him before.

97. Here is a beautiful instance of a setter's untutor-
ed intelligence, leading her to see the advantage of

having running birds between herself and the gun. On gaining some high ground, the dog drew and stood. She was walked up to, but, to my astonishment, we found no birds. She was encouraged, and, with much difficulty, coaxed off her point. She kept drawing on, but with the same ill success. I must confess I was for the moment sorely puzzled, but knowing the excellence of the animal, I left her alone. She kept drawing on,—but still no birds. At last, of her own accord, and with a degree of instinct amounting almost to the faculty of reasoning, she broke from her point, and dashing off to the right, made a " détour," and was presently straight before me, some three hundred yards off, setting the game, whatever it might be; as much as to say, "escape me this time!" We walked steadily on, and when within about thirty yards of her, up got a covey of red-legged partridges.

98. A gentleman had a pointer so fleet that he often backed him to find birds in a ten acre field within two minutes, if there were birds in it. On entering the field, he seemed to know by instinct where the birds would be, generally going up to them at once. His nose was so good, that, with a brisk wind, he would find his game a hundred and fifty yards off across the furrows. He could tell whether a bird was hit, and if so, would retrieve it some fields off from where it was shot. He would never follow a hare, unless it was wounded. He would point water-fowl as well as all birds of game; and has been seen pointing a duck or a moor-hen with the water running over his back at the time. Nothing seemed to spoil this dog, not even rat

2 H

or otter hunting, in both of which he was an adept, as
he knew his business; and, although he would rattle
through a wood, he was perfectly steady the next
minute out of cover. He has been known to continue
at a point two hours. In high turnips he would con-
trive to show his master where he was, standing sometimes on his hind legs only, so that his head and
forequarters might be seen. On one occasion, he came
at full speed so suddenly on a hare, that he slipped up,
and fell nearly on his back. In this position he did
not move, and it was thought he was in a fit, till the
hare jumped up and was killed, when the dog righted
himself. So steady was he in backing another dog
when game was found, that he once caught sight of a
point at the moment of jumping a stile, and balanced
himself on it for several seconds till he fell. Once,
when hunting with a young pointer, who had only been
taken into the field two or three times, in order to
shew him some birds before the shooting season, the
following occurrence took place. The old dog found
some birds in the middle of the field, and pointed
them steadily. The puppy had been jumping and
gambolling about, with no great hunt in him, and,
upon seeing the old dog stand, ran playfully up to him.
He was, however, seized by the neck, and received a
good shaking, which sent him away howling; and his
companion then turned round and steadied himself
on his point, without moving scarcely a yard.

99. On one occasion, when a relation of mine was shooting on the banks of the Forth, he killed a partridge that
was flying across the river. As he had no retriever

with him, he almost regretted having fired ; but, to his surprise, his setter, Dove, jumped into the river, although she had never previously (to the writer's knowledge) attempted to swim, seized it, and deposited it safely on the bank.

100. I was with a gentleman, who resides in the country, in his study, when a pointer dog belonging to him came running to the door of the room, which was shut, scratching and barking till he was admitted. He then used supplicating gestures of every kind, running from his master to the stair, behind which his gun stood, then again to his master, and back to the gun. The gentleman now comprehended something of his dog's meaning, and took up his gun. The dog immediately gave a bark of joy, ran to the back door of the house, from whence he took the road to a neighbouring hill. His master and I followed him. The dog ran, highly pleased, a little distance before us, showing us the way we should take. After we had proceeded about forty paces, he gave us to understand that we should turn to the left, by pressing repeatedly against his master, and pushing him towards the road that turned to the left. We followed his direction, and he accompanied us a few paces, but suddenly he turned to the right, running round the whole of the hill. We still proceeded to the left, slowly up the ascent, till we were nearly arrived at its summit ; the dog, in the meantime, making the circuit of the hill to the right. He was now already higher than we were, when he gave a sudden bark, and that moment a hare ran before the muzzle of his master's gun, and of course met her fate.

101. During my residence in the country, I had a
gamekeeper who was very skilful in the art of training
dogs. Among others of various kinds which he trained,
was a large old English setter, with which he had
succeeded so well, that he could use him both for
hunting and shooting. This dog did always as much
as could be done by any of his race, in whatever kind
of sport he was employed; he even invented advantageous manœuvres himself which the gamekeeper
affirmed he had never taught him. Once, after I had
been already several hours returned from hunting with
my people, the dog came running across the yard with
a hare upon his back, which he held by the ear, so as
to carry her in the most convenient manner to the
kitchen, from the considerable distance where he must
have killed her. Upon another occasion, he showed an
extraordinary degree of judgment and fidelity. The
gamekeeper had, on one of the short days of December,
shot at and wounded a deer. Hoping to run him
down before night, he instantly put the dog on the
track, which followed it at full speed, and soon was
out of sight, At length it grew dark, and the gamekeeper returned home, thinking he should find the
setter arrived there before him; but he was disappointed, and became apprehensive that his dog might have
lost himself, or fallen a prey to some ravenous animal.
The next morning, however, we were all greatly
rejoiced to see him come running into the yard, when
he directly hastened to the door of my apartment, and,
on being admitted, ran with gestures expressive of
solicitude and eagerness to a corner of the room where

guns were placed. We understood the hint, and, taking
the guns, followed. He led us, not by the road which
he himself had taken out of the wood, but by beaten
paths half round it, and then by several wood-cutter's
tracks in different directions to a thicket, where,
following him a few paces, we found the deer which
he had killed. The dog seems to have rightly judged
that we should have been obliged to make our way
with much difficulty through almost the whole length
of the wood, in order to come to the deer in a straight
direction, and he therefore led us a circuitous, but
open and convenient road Between the legs of the
deer, which he had guarded during the night against
the beasts of prey that might otherwise have seized
upon it, he had scratched a hole in the snow, and filled
it with dry leaves for his bed. The extraordinary
sagacity which he had displayed upon this occasion,
rendered him doubly valuable to us; and it therefore
caused us very serious regret, when, in the ensuing
summer, the poor animal went mad, possibly in consequence of his exposure to the severe frost of that
night; and it became necessary for the gamekeeper to
shoot him, which he could not do without shedding
tears. He said he could willingly have given his best
cow to save him; and I confess myself that I would
not have hesitated to part with my best horse upon the
same terms.

102. A gentleman had a favourite spaniel, which, for
a long time, was in the habit of accompanying him in
all his walks, and became his attached companion.
This gentleman had occasion to leave home, and was

absent for more than a year, during which time he had never seen the dog. On his return, along with a friend, while yet at a little distance from the house, they perceived the spaniel lying beside the gate. He thought that this would be a good opportunity for testing the memory of his favourite ; and he accordingly arranged with his companion, who was quite unknown to the dog, that they should both walk up to the animal and express no signs of recognition. As they both approached nearer, the dog started up, and gazed at them attentively, but he discovered no signs of recognition at their near approach. At last he came up to the stranger, put his nose close to his clothes, and smelt him, without any signs of emotion. He then did the same to his old master; but no sooner had he smelt him, than recognition instantly took place: he leaped up to his face repeatedly, and showed symptoms of extravagant joy. He followed him into the house and watched his every movement, and could by no means be diverted from his person. Here was an instance of deficient memory through the organs of sight, but an accurate recollection through the organs of smell.

103. The modes employed by dogs of different races in capturing and devouring the crab, and especially that pugnacious species, the velvet-crab, will illustrate the experience which has become propagated in the breed, over the ignorance of the uninitiated. On the first discovery of the prey, a terrier runs in to seize it, and is immediately and severely bitten on the nose. But a sedate Newfoundland dog of my acquaintance, proceeds more soberly in his work. He lays his paw

on it, to arrest it in its escape; then, tumbling it over, he bares his teeth, and, seizing it with the mouth, throws the crab aloft: it falls upon the stones; the shell is cracked beyond redemption; and then the dainty dish is devoured at his leisure.

104. If we admit that dogs possess the faculty of thought, here is a decided case of a dog dying of a broken heart:—A poor tailor of the Borough left a small dog inconsolable for his loss. The little animal would not leave his dead master even for his food; and when the corpse was removed for burial, he followed the mournful train to the church-yard, and would have remained at the grave but for the sexton, whose ruder sensibilities prompted his expulsion. He was found the next day on the grave of his master, and there continued to repeat his visit as often was he expelled, till, one day the circumstance having become known to the clergyman, he had him supplied daily with food, and even built him a kennel on the spot, in order that he might indulge the bent of his inclination. Two years did this mirror of fidelity pass in this manner, till death put an end to his griefs.

105. Opposite to the home of a gentlemen, near the church-yard of St. Olave, in Southwark, and where the little receptacles of humanity are in many parts dilapidated, was an aperture just large enough to admit a dog. It led along a kind of sink to a dark cavity, close to which a person had lately been buried. It was inhabited by his dog, who was to be seen occasionally moving into or out of the cavern. He had taken possession of it on the day of the funeral. How he

obtained any food during the first two or three months,
no one knew; but he at length attracted the attention of
a gentleman who lived opposite, and who ordered his
servant regularly to supply the poor fellow.  He used,
after awhile, to come occasionally to this house for the
food that was provided for him.  He was not sullen,
but there was a melancholy expression in his countenance, which, once observed, could never be forgotten.
As soon as he had finished his hasty meal, he would
gaze for a moment on his benefactor.  It was an expressive look, and which could not be misunderstood.
It conveyed all the thanks that a broken heart could
give.  He then entombed himself once more for three
or four days, when he crawled out again with his eyes
sunk and his coat dishevelled.  Two years he was
faithful to the memory of him whom he had lost ; and
then, according to the most authentic account of him,
having been missing several days, he was found dead
in his retreat.

106. One day, when Dumont, a tradesman of the
Rue St. Denis, was walking in the Boulvard St. Antoine
with a friend, he offered to lay a wager with the latter
that if he were to hide a six-Louis d'or piece in the dust,
his dog would discover and bring it to him.  The wager
was accepted, and the piece of money secreted after
having been carefully marked.  When the two had
proceeded some distance from the spot, M. Dumont
called to his dog that he had lost something, and
ordered him to seek it.  Caniche immediately turned
back, and his master and his companion pursued their
walk to the Rue St. Denis.  Meanwhile, a traveller, who

happened to be just then returning in a small chaise from
Vincennes, perceived the piece of money which his horse
had kicked from its hiding-place. He alighted, took it
up, and drove to his inn in the Rue Pont aux-Choux.
Caniche had just reached the spot in search of the lost
piece, when the stranger picked it up. He followed
the chaise, went into the inn, and stuck close to the
traveller. Having scented out the coin which he had
been ordered to bring back in the pocket of the latter,
he leaped up incessantly at and about him, the traveller
supposing him to be some dog that had been lost or
left behind by his master, regarded his different movements as marks of fondness; and, as the animal was
very handsome, he determined to keep him He gave
him a good supper, and on retiring to bed, took him
with him to his chamber. No sooner had he pulled off
his clothes than they were seized by the dog; the
owner, conceiving that he wanted to play with them,
took them away again. The animal began to bark at
the door, which the traveller opened, under the idea
that the dog wanted to go out. Caniche snatched up
the clothes, and away he flew. The traveller posted
after him with his night cap on, and literally sans
culottes. Anxiety for the fate of a purse full of gold
Napoleons, of forty francs each, gave redoubled velocity
to his steps. Caniche ran full speed to his master's
house, where the stranger arrived a moment afterwards,
breathless and enraged. He accused the dog of robbing
him. " Sir," said the master, " my dog is a faithful
creature, and if he has run away with your trousers,
it is because you have in them money which does not

belong to you. The traveller became still more exasperated. " Compose yourself, sir," rejoined he, smiling :
" without doubt there is in your pocket a six-Louis d'or
piece, with such and such marks, which you have
picked up in the Boulevard St. Antoine, and which I
threw down there with the firm conviction that my dog
would bring it back again. This is the cause of the
robbery he has committed upon you." The stranger's
rage now yielded to astonishment : he delivered the
six-Louis d'or piece to the owner, and could not forbear
caressing the dog which had given him so much uneasiness, and such an unpleasant chase.

107. A most extraordinary circumstance has just
occurred at the Hawick toll-bar, which is kept by two
old women. It appears that they had a sum of money
in the house, and were extremely alarmed lest they
should be robbed of it. Their fears prevailed to such
an extent, that when a carrier whom they knew was
passing by, they urgently requested him to remain
with them all night, which, however, his duties would
not permit him to do ; but, in consideration of the
alarm of the women, he consented to leave with them
a large mastiff dog. In the night the women were
disturbed by the uneasiness of the dog, and heard a
noise apparently like an attempt to force an entrance
into the premises, upon which they escaped by the
back door, and ran to a neighbouring house, which
happened to be blacksmith's shop. They knocked at
the door and were answered from within by the smith's
wife ; she said her husband was absent, but that she
was willing to accompany the terrified women to their

home. On reaching the house, they heard a savage but half-stifled growling from the dog. On entering, they saw the body of a man hanging half in and half out of their window, whom the dog had seized by the throat, and was still worrying. On examination, the man proved to be their neighbour the blacksmith, dreadfully torn about the throat, and quite dead.

108. The Newfoundland dog has a sagacity that is remarkably strong and humane in its character. This animal appears as if designed to be a companion to man, but more particularly when he is exposed to the perils of the water. With semi-webbed feet, which make him a good swimmer, and an inclination to enter the water, this element seems half natural to his nature. It is when persons are in the act of drowning that the sagacity of this dog displays itself more strongly, and innumerable lives has it saved from a watery grave. One instance will serve our purpose as well as a hundred which might be enumerated. A singular case is given of a person who was travelling in Holland, and accompanied by a Newfoundland dog. Not taking proper heed to his steps in an evening walk along a high bank by the side of one of those canals common in the country, his foot slipped, letting him into the deep with a plunge ; and being unable to swim, the fish's element soon deprived him of his senses. In the mean time, the sagacious animal had no sooner discovered the danger to which his master was exposed, than he was in the water, and engaged in the struggle to rescue him from his peril. A party at a distance saw the faithful servant at one moment

pushing, and at another dragging the body towards a small creek, when, at length, he succeeded in landing his charge, and placing it as far from the water as possible. This being done, the dog first shook himself, and then licked the hands and face of his apparently dead lord. The body being conveyed to a neighbouring house, the efforts to restore the lost senses were successful.

108. Dr. Beattie, in one of his elegant essays, relates a transaction within his own knowledge, of a gentleman's life being saved who fell beneath the ice, by his dog going in search of assistance, and almost forcibly draging a farmer to the scene of anxiety and expectation.

109. M. Valliant feelingly describes the loss of a setter dog during his travels in Africa, when, after repeatedly firing his gun, and every fruitless search for her, he dispatched one of his attendants to return by the way they had proceeded, when she was found at about two leagues distance, seated by the side of a chair and basket which had dropped unperceived from the waggon; an instance of attentive fidelity which must have proved fatal to the animal, either from hunger or beasts of prey, had she not been luckily discovered.

110. It was with pleasure that I watched the motions of a grateful animal belonging to one of the workmen employed at Portsmouth dock-yard. This man had a large cur dog, who regularly every day brought him his dinner upwards of a mile. When his wife had prepared the repast, she tied it up in a cloth, and put it in a hand-basket. Then calling Trusty, (for so he was

properly named) desired him to be expeditious, and carry his master's dinner, and be sure not to stop by the way. The dog, who perfectly understood his orders, immediately obeyed by taking the handle of the basket in his mouth, and began his journey. It was laughable to observe that, when tired by the way, he would very cautiously set the basket on the ground, but by no means would suffer any person to come near it. When he had sufficiently rested himself, he again took up his load, and proceeded forward until he came to the dock gates. Here he was frequently obliged to stop, and wait with patience until the porter or some other person opened the door. His joy was then visible to every one. His pace increased, and with wagging tail, expressive of his pleasure, he ran to his master with the refreshment. The caresses were then mutual, and, after receiving his morsel as a recompense for his fidelity, he was ordered home with the empty basket and plates, which he carried back with the greatest precision, to the high diversion of all spectators.

111. One of the most interesting anecdotes I have known relates to a sheep dog. The names of the parties have escaped me just now, but I recollect perfectly that it came from an authentic source. The circumstances were these :—A gentleman sold a considerable flock of sheep to a dealer, which the latter had not hands to drive. The seller, however, told him he had a very intelligent dog which he could send to assist him to a place about thirty miles off, and that, when he reached the end of his journey, he had only

I

to feed the dog, and desire him to go home. The dog
accordingly received his orders, and set off with the
flock and the drover. But he was absent for so many
days that his master began to have serious alarms
about him, when, one morning to his great surprise, he
found the dog returned with a very large flock of sheep,
including the whole that he had lately sold. The fact
turned out to be, that the drover was so pleased with
the colley that he resolved to steal him, and locked
him up until the time when he was to leave the country.
The dog grew sulky, and made various attempts to
escape; and one evening he fortunately succeeded.
Whether the brute had discovered the drover's intention, and supposed the sheep were also stolen, it is
difficult to say, but by his conduct it looked so; for he
immediately went to the field, collected the sheep, and
drove them all back to his master.

112. A few years ago, when upon a shooting party in
the braes of Rannoch, the dogs were so worn out as to
be unfit for travel. Our guide said he knew a
shepherd who had a dog that perhaps might help us.
He called, and the young man came with his little
black colley, to which, as soon as he had conversed
with the guide, he said something in Erse. The dog
set off in a sneaking sort of manner up the hill, and
when he showed any degree of keenness, we hastened
to follow, lest he should set up the birds; but the lad
advised us to be canny, as it was time eneuh when
Lud came back to tell. In a short space, Lud made
his appearance on a knoll, and sat down; and the
shepherd said we might go up now, for Lud had found

the birds. The dog waited till we were ready, and trotted on at his master's command, who soon cautioned us to be on the alert, for Lud signified we were in the midst of the covey. We immediately found this to be the case, and in the course of the day the same thing occurred frequently.

113. I was once called from dinner in a hurry to attend to something that had occurred. Unintentionally I left a favourite cat in the room, together with a no less favourite spaniel. When I returned, I found the latter, which was not a small figure, extending her whole length along the table, by the side of a leg of mutton which I had left. On my entrance she showed no signs of fear, nor did she immediately alter her position. I was sure, therefore, that none but a good motive had placed her in this extraordinary situation, nor had I long to conjecture. Puss was skulking in a corner, and though the mutton was untouched, yet her conscious fears clearly evinced that she had been driven from the table in the act of attempting a robbery on the meat, to which she was too prone, and that her situation had been occupied by this faithful spaniel to prevent a repetition of the attempt. Here was fidelity united with great intellect, and wholly free from the aid of instinct. This property of guarding victuals from the cat, or from other dogs, was a daily practice with this animal, and while cooking was going forward, the floor might be strewed with eatables, which would have been all safe from her own touch, and as carefully guarded from that of others. A similar property is common to many dogs, but to spaniels particularly.

114. I recollect when I passed some time at the Viscount Arbuthot's, at Hatton, in the parish of Mary-kirk, one of his lordship's estates, that when the field servants went out one morning, they found a man whom they knew, and who lived a few miles distance, lying on the road a short way from the stable with a number of bridles, girths, &c. near him, and the house dog, which was of the Highland breed, lying also at his ease, holding the man by his trowsers. The man confessed his crime, and told them that the dog had struggled with him, and held him in that position for five hours; but that immediately after the servants came up he let go his hold.

115. Not long ago, a young man, an acquaintance of Lord Fife's coachman, was walking, as he had often done, in his lordship's stables at Banff. Taking an opportunity when the servants were not regarding him, he put a bridle into his pocket. A Highland cur that was generally about the stables observed the theft, and immediately began to bark at him; and when he got to the stable door, would not let him pass, but held him fiercely by the leg to prevent him. As the servants had never seen the dog act thus before; and the same young man had been often with them, they could not imagine what could be the reason of the dog's conduct. However, when they perceived the end of a valuable bridle peeping out of the young man's pocket, they were able to account for it; and on his giving it up, the dog let go his hold, and allowed him to pass.

116. In October, 1800, a young man going into a place of public entertainment at Paris, was told that

his dog could not be permitted to enter; and he was accordingly left with the guard at the door. The young man had scarcely entered into the lobby, when his watch was stolen. He returned to the guard, and prayed that his dog might be admitted, as through his means he might be enabled to discover the thief. The dog was permitted to accompany his master, who, by signal, intimated to the animal what he had lost. The dog immediately set out in quest of the *strayed* article, and soon fastened on the thief, whose guilt, upon searching him, soon became apparent. The fellow proved an old offender, six watches were found in his pockets, which, being laid before the dog, he most sagaciously selected his master's, took it in his mouth, and bore it in safety to his master.

# THE ELEPHANT.

———•┼┊•·———

Reasoning at every step he treads,
Man yet mistakes his way;
While meaner things whom instinct leads,
Are rarely known to stray.—Cowper.

117. Observe one walking. You will see that his
trunk oscillates like a pendulum, and touches the
ground between each paw. Though seemingly a chance
matter, it is not so, for by this slight touch the elephant
judges whether the place where he will next place his
foot is equal to bearing his weight or no, and he is
very seldom mistaken on this point. If the trunk gets
injured, this, however, ceases, (I suppose from the
nerves being partially or wholly destroyed) and the
animal becomes useless in unsafe ground, and troublesome to drive, as he resists going over bridges and
other places, which, though really safe, he is not sure
of. So well aware is the elephant of the value of his
trunk, that his first care, on the approach of danger, is
to elevate it over his head out of harm's way.

118. A friend of the Messrs. Chambers, of Edinburgh,
gives the following account of the capture of wild
elephants by means of tame ones :—" Having thus so
far succeeded, the next thing was to secure them, and
for this purpose the tame elephants were introduced

into the kraal. Six very large ones were brought in,
just under our tree, and began breaking down the
jungle, and clearing a space round the large trees, to
which it was intended to tie the wild ones. It was
really wonderful to see them twining their trunks
round some of the smaller trees, and with two or three
good shakes laying them flat. They sometimes pushed
their head against a tree, so as to bring the whole
force of their body upon it, and then down it came;
as for the brushwood, part of which was upwards of
six feet high, they really mowed it down with their
trunks. In about an hour's time, the whole was,
comparatively speaking, clear, and the poor herd had
no longer any hiding-place, but stood all huddled close
together in a little thicket about the middle of the
kraal. There was one very little thing among them,
not much bigger than a large pig, and they seemed
to take the greatest care of him, keeping him in the
centre of them. Each tame elephant had two men on
his back, one to guide him, and the other to noose the
wild ones, who did not seem to be much afraid of
them, as they allowed them to come very near, and
then walked rather slowly away. One of the tame ones
then followed, in the most stealthy and treacherous
manner possible, and when he came close enough to
the wild one, he began coaxing him and tickling him
with his trunk, whilst the man with the noose, which
is fastened round the tame one's neck, slipped off his
back with it, and watched his opportunity to throw it
over the hind leg of the other. He soon did this, as
apparently the tame one gave the wild elephant a poke

with his tusk, which made him lift his leg as if to move
on; and in a moment he was a prisoner. While the
man was thus employed, it was curious to see the care
which the tame elephant took of him, interposing his
huge head in such a manner that the wild one could
not touch him; and, if he should fail of securing the
wild elephant, which sometimes happens, the tame one
puts out his leg for the man to mount on his back, and
sets off in pursuit again, which is sure to be successful
in the end. When the poor animal was noosed, he set
up a dreadful yell, and tried to escape; but that was
impossible, for the other tame elephants came up and
headed him, whichever way he attempted to go; whilst
the one to which he was fastened, bent his body the way
he wished to take him, and pulled him along with all
his strength to the tree to which he was to be tied.
When he was dragged close to it, the tame one walked
round it two or three times with the rope, till he was
quite secure. Another came to his other side, and
thus he was wedged so closely between them, that he
could not make much resistance; and if he did, he
was immediately thrust at with the tusks of both of
them. In this way his legs were all firmly tied to two
trees by great cable ropes. When the tame ones left
him to go in search of the others, he began struggling
most furiously, and moaned and bellowed in a very
melancholy manner, frequently throwing himself on
the ground, and digging his teeth into the earth, while
the tears were rolling down his face. Although I came
on purpose to see all this, and should have been much
disappointed if I had not, still I could not help feeling

very sorry to see the noble animal suffering so acutely. My consolation was, that some day he would have the pleasure of doing the same to others; for it really seemed a pleasure to the tame ones. His cries brought back the rest of the herd, who looked at him through the bushes, but did not attempt a rescue, which they often do, but took to their heels whenever they saw the tames ones turn in their direction. In this manner they were all secured, except the little one, as he could not do much harm, and always kept close to his mother. who was very quiet, and was therefore only tied by three legs. A young elephant is, I think, the drollest looking creature possible. This one was supposed to be about three months old, and was not above three feet high; but it made more noise than all the rest, and trumpeted and charged in great style.

119. Even in our country the elephant has been taught to take part in the performances of the theatre—in other words, to appear as an actor requisite to the plot of the drama. This took place in the London Adelphi and in the Coburg, about twelve or fourteen years ago; and however questionable might have been the taste, there is no doubt that the " sagacious brute" was the most applauded player of the time. This animal, a female, was marched in procession, knelt down at the waving of the hand, placed the crown on the head of "the true prince," uncorked and drank several bottles of wine with decorum, supped with her state companions around her, and made her obeisance to the audience. Above all, she assisted in the escape of some of the *dramatis personæ* from prison, by kneeling upon her

hind legs, and thus forming an inclined plane for the
safe descent of her friends; and this she did, unmoved
by the glare of numerous lights, the sounds of music,
and shouts of the admiring spectators. Equally curious
with this is the feat mentioned by Arrian, of an elephant
that he saw beating a measure with cymbals. This was
performed by having two cymbals attached to its knees,
while it held a third in its proboscis, and beat with
great exactness the while others danced around it,
without deviating from the time indicated. Busbequius,
who visited Constantinople about the middle of the
sixteenth century, there witnessed an elephant not only
dance with elegance and accuracy, but play at ball with
great skill, tossing it with his trunk, and catching it
again, as easily as a man could with his hands. If we
can credit Ælian, he has seen an elephant "write Latin
characters on a board in a very orderly manner, his
keeper only showing him the figure of each letter."

120. Among the most interesting elephants kept in
this country, without any reference to profit, was one
which was lately at the Duke of Devonshire's villa, at
Chiswick, the gift of a lady in India. This animal was
a female, remarkable for the gentleness of its disposition; and from the kindness with which it was treated,
and the free range that was allowed it, probably came
nearer to an elephant in a state of nature than any
other which ever appeared in this country. The house
erected for her shelter was of large dimensions, and
well ventilated; and she had, besides, the range of a
paddock of considerable extent. At the call of her
keeper she came out of her house, and immediately

took up a broom, ready to perform his bidding in sweeping the grass or paths. She would follow him with a pail or watering-pot round the enclosure. Her reward was a carrot and some water; but previously to satisfying her thirst, she would exhibit her ingenuity by emptying the contents of a' soda water bottle, which was tightly corked. This she did by pressing the bottle against the ground with her foot, so as to hold it securely at an angle of about forty-five degrees, and gradually twisting out the cork with her trunk, although it was very little above the edge of the neck; then, without altering the position, she turned her trunk round the bottle, so that she might reverse it, and thus empty the contents into the extremity of the proboscis. This she accomplished without spilling a drop, and she delivered the empty bottle to her keeper before she attempted to discharge the contents of the trunk into her mouth. The affection of this poor animal for her keeper was so great, that she would cry after him whenever he was absent for more than a few hours. She was about twenty-nine years old when she died, early in 1820, of what was understood to be pulmonary consumption. It is not always, however, for mere amusement or curiosity that the docility of the elephant is exhibited : it would say little for human ingenuity, were not the strength of such a powerful animal brought to bear upon useful and necessary operations. We have seen that in India he is made a beast of carriage and draught, carrying indifferently the howdah and baggage chest, and dragging the ponderous artillery-car;

but besides this, there are many other minor occupations
in which he can be successfully engaged.

121. Elephants were at one time employed in the
launching of ships, being trained to push in unison
with their powerful fronts and heavy bodies.  It is told
of one that was directed to force a large vessel into the
water, but which proved superior to his strength, that,
on being upbraided for his laziness, the distressed
animal increased his efforts with such vehemence, that
he fractured his skull on the spot.

122. I have seen two occupied in beating down a wall
which their keepers had desired them to do, and encouraged them by a promise of fruit and brandy.  They
combined their efforts; and doubling up their trunks,
which were guarded from injury by leather, thrust
against the strongest part of the wall, and by reiterated
shocks continued their attacks, still observing and
following the effect of the equilibrium with their eyes;
then at last making one grand effort, they suddenly
drew back together, that they might not be wounded
by the ruins.

123. It is also told of an elephant at Barrackpoor,
that he would swim laden with parcels to the opposite
shore of the Ganges, and then unload himself with
undeviating accuracy.

124. In the year 1811, a lady, staying with her
husband, an officer in the Company's service, at a house
near the fort of Travancore, was astonished one morning
to observe an elephant, unattended, marching into the
courtyard, carrying a box in his trunk, apparently very
heavy.  He deposited this, and going his way, soon

returned with a similar box, which he placed by the
side of the other. He continued this operation till he
had formed a considerable pile, arranged with undeviating order The boxes contained the treasure of the
rajah of Travancore, who had died in the night, and of
whose property the English commander had taken
possession, thus removing the more valuable part for
greater security.

125. I have myself seen the wife of a mahoud (for
the followers often take their families with them to
camp) give a baby in charge to an elephant, while she
went on some business, and have been highly amused
in observing the sagacity and care of the unwieldy
nurse. The child, which, like most children, did not
like to lie still in one position, would, as soon as left to
itself, begin crawling about; in which exercise it would
probably get among the legs of the animal, or entangled
in the branches of the trees on which he was feeding;
when the elephant would, in the most tender manner,
disengage his charge, either by lifting it out of the way
with his trunk, or by removing the impediments to its
free progress. If the child had crawled to such a
distance as to verge upon the limits of his range (for
the animal was chained by the leg to a peg driven into
the ground), he would stretch out his trunk, and lift it
back as gently as possible to the spot whence it started.

125. Dr. Darwin tells us, that he was informed by a
gentleman of veracity, that in some parts of the East
the elephant is taught to walk on a narrow path between
two pitfalls which are covered with turf, and then to go
into the woods and induce the wild herd to come that

way. The decoy walks slowly onward till near the trap,
and then bustles away as if in sport or in fear, passing
safely between the pits, while some of those which
follow in the wake are inevitably entangled. The same
gentleman says also, that it was universally observed
that such wild elephants as had escaped the snare,
always pursued the traitor with the utmost vehemence;
and if they could overtake him, which sometimes
happened, they beat him to death.

126. In the Philosophical Transactions, a story is
related of a elephant having such an attachment for a
very young child, that he was never happy but when
it was near him. The nurse used, therefore, very
frequently to take the child in its cradle and place it
between its feet. This he at length became so accustomed to, that he would never eat his food except when
it was present. When the child slept, he used to drive
off the flies with his proboscis; and when it cried, he
would move the cradle backwards and forwards, and
thus rock it again to sleep. Nor will this instance of
sagacious affection appear at all improbable to those
who are acquainted with the thorough intimacy which
generally subsists between the family of the. Indian
mahoud and his elephant, which may be said literally
to live under the same roof, eat the same bread, and
drink the same water

127. The following instances of gratitude are in the
highest degree praiseworthy, and might well put to the
blush many who lay claim to a higher position in the
scale of intelligence:—An elephant in Ajmeer, which
passed frequently through the bazaar, or market, as he

went by a certain herb woman, always received from her a mouthful of greens. At length he was seized with one of his periodical fits of rage, broke from his fetters, and, running through the market, put the crowd to flight, and among others this woman, who in her haste forgot a little child she had brought with her. The animal, gratefully recollecting the spot where his benefactress was wont to sit, laid aside his fury, and taking up the infant gently in his trunk, placed it safely on a stall before a neighbouring house.

128. There was a soldier at Pondicherry who was accustomed, whenever he received his share of liquor, to carry a certain quantity of it to one of these animals, and by this means a very cordial intimacy was formed between them. Having drunk rather too freely one day, and finding himself pursued by the guards, who were going to take him to prison, the soldier took refuge under the elephant's body, and fell asleep. The guard tried in vain to force him from this asylum, as the animal protected him most strenuously with his trunk. The following morning, the soldier, recovering from his drunken fit, shuddered with horror to find himself stretched under this huge animal. The elephant, who, without doubt, perceived the man's embarrassment, caressed him with his trunk, in order to inspire him with courage, and made him understand that he might now depart in safety.

129. Every one must have read of the mishaps of the Delhi tailor. This individual was in the habit of giving some little delicacy, such as an apple, to an elephant that daily passed by his shop, and so accustomed had

the animal become to this treatment, that it regularly put its trunk in at the window to receive the expected gift. One day, however, the tailor being out of humour, thrust his needle into the beast's proboscis, telling it to be gone, as he had nothing to give it. The creature passed on, apparently unmoved; but on coming to the next dirty pool of water, filled its trunk, and returned to the shop-window, into which it discharged the whole contents, thoroughly drenching poor Snip and the wares by which he was surrounded. Again, a painter was desirous of drawing the elephant kept in the menagerie at Versailles in an uncommon attitude, which was that of holding its trunk raised in the air, with his mouth open. The painter's boy, in order to keep the animal in this posture, threw fruit into his mouth; but as he had frequently deceived him, and made him an offer only of throwing the fruit, he grew angry; and, as if he had known the painter's intention of drawing him was the cause of the affront that was offered him, instead of revenging himself on the lad, he turned his resentment on the master, and taking up a quantity of water in his trunk, threw it on the paper which the painter was drawing on, and spoilt it.

130. A sentinel belonging to the present menagerie at Paris was always very careful in requesting the spectators not to give the elephant anything to eat. This conduct particularly displeased the female, who beheld him with a very unfavourable eye, and had several times endeavoured to correct his interference by sprinkling his head with water from her trunk. One day, when several persons were collected to view these

animals, a bystander offered the female a bit of bread. The sentinel perceived it; but the moment he opened his mouth to give his usual admonition, she, placing herself immediately before him, discharged in his face a violent stream of water. A general laugh ensued; but the sentinel having calmly wiped his face, stood a little to one side, and continued as vigilant as before. Soon afterwards he found himself under the necessity of repeating his admonition to the spectators, but no sooner was this uttered, than the female laid hold of his musket, twirled it round with her trunk, trod it under her feet, and did not restore it till she had twisted it nearly into the form of a cork-screw.

131. It is stated, amongst the traditionary stories of elephant resentment, that Pidcock, to whom the Exeter 'Change menagerie formerly belonged, had for some years a custom of treating himself and his elephant in the evening with a glass of spirits, for which the animal regularly looked. Pidcock invariably gave the elephant the first glass out of the bottle, till one night he exclaimed, " You have been served first long enough, and it's my turn now." The proud beast was offended, refused the glass when he was denied the precedence, and never more would join his master in his revelries.

132. An elephant that was exhibited in France some years ago, seemed to know when it was mocked by any person, and remembered the affront till an opportunity for revenge occurred. A man deceived it, by pretending to throw something into its mouth: the animal gave him such a blow with his trunk as knocked him down, and broke two of his ribs; after which it trampled upon

K

him, broke one of his legs, and bending down on its knees, endeavoured to push its tusks into his body, but they luckily ran into the ground on each side of his thigh, without doing him any injury.

133. At Macassar an elephant driver had a cocoa nut given him, which, out of wantonness, he struck twice against his elephant's head to break. The following day, the animal saw some cocoa nuts exposed in the street for sale, and taking one of them up with his trunk, beat it about the driver's head till the man was dead.

134. Recently, at Liverpool Zoological Gardens, after delighting groups of young holiday folks by his skilful and docile performances, the elephant gave some offence to one of the deputy-keepers, and was by him chastised with a broomstick. No one was by to see what occurred in the next few minutes; but at the expiration of that time, the unfortunate deputy-keeper was found dead at the feet of the insulted beast, having been killed, in all probability, by a single blow of the animal's trunk. The body presented a most appalling spectacle, the arms and legs being fractured in several places, the skull cloven, and the entire body crushed to pieces by the animal, who, it would appear, in his rage, had repeatedly trampled upon him.

135. A female elephant that had escaped to the forest, and had enjoyed her liberty for more than ten years, was at last caught, along with a number of others, in a keddah. After the others had been secured, with the exception of seven or eight young ones, the hunters, who recognised this female, were ordered to call on her

by name. She immediately came to the side of the
ditch within the enclosure, on which some of the
drivers were desired to carry a plantain tree, the
leaves of which she not only took from their hands
with her trunk, but opened her mouth for them to put
a leaf into it, which they did, stroking and caressing
her, and calling to her by name. One of the trained
elephants was now ordered to be brought to her, and
the driver to take her by the ear and order her to lie
down. At first she did not like the koomkee to go near
her, and retired to a distance, seeming angry; but when
the drivers, who were on foot, called to her, she came
immediately, and allowed them to stroke and caress
her as before, and in a few minutes after, permitted
the trained elephants to be familiar. A driver from one
of these then fastened a rope round her body, and
instantly jumped on her back, which at the moment
she did not like, but was soon reconciled to it. A small
cord was then put round her neck for the driver to put
his feet in, who, seating himself on the neck in the
usual manner, drove her about the enclosure in the
same manner as any of the tame elephants. After this
he ordered her to lie down, which she instantly did;
nor did she rise till she was desired. He fed her from
his seat. gave her his stick to hold, which she took with
her trunk and put into her mouth. kept, and then
returned it as she was directed, and as she had formerly
been accustomed to do. In short, she was so obedient,
that had there been more wild elephants in the enclosure, she would have been useful in securing them.

136. In June 1787, a male elephant, taken .the year before, was travelling, in company with some others, towards Chittagong, laden with baggage, and having come on a tiger's track, which elephants discover readily by the smell, he took fright and ran off to the woods, in spite of all the efforts of his driver. On entering the wood, the driver saved himself by springing from the animal, and clinging to the branch of a tree under which he was passing. When the elephant had got rid of his driver, he soon contrived to shake off his load. As soon as he ran away, a trained female was despatched after him, but could not get up in time to prevent his escape. Eighteen months after this, when a herd of elephants had been taken, and had remained several days in the enclosure till they were enticed into the outlet, there tied, and led out in the usual manner, one of the drivers, viewing a male elephant very attentively, declared he resembled the one which had run away. This excited the curiosity of every one to go and look at him; but when any person came near, the animal struck at him with his trunk, and in every respect appeared as wild and outrageous as any of the other elephants. An old hunter at length coming up and examining him, declared that he was the very elephant that had made his escape. Confident of this, he boldly rode up to him on a tame elephant, and ordered him to lie down, pulling him by the ear at the same time. The animal seemed taken by surprise, and instantly obeyed the word of command, uttering at the same time a peculiar shrill squeak through his trunk, as he had formerly been known to do, by which he was imme-

diately recognised by every person who was acquainted with this peculiarity. Thus we see that this elephant, for the space of eight or ten days, during which he was in the enclosure, appeared equally wild and fierce with the boldest elephant then taken; but the moment he was addressed in a commanding tone, the recollection of his former obedience seemed to rush upon him at once, and, without any difficulty, he permitted a driver to be seated on his neck, who in a few days made him as tractable as ever.

137. A female elephant belonging to a gentleman in Calcutta being ordered from the upper country to Chotygoné, by chance broke loose from her keeper, and was lost in the woods. The excuses which the keeper made were not admitted. It was supposed that he had sold the elephant: his wife and family therefore were sold for slaves, and he was himself condemned to work upon the roads. About twelve years afterwards, this man was ordered up into the country to assist in catching the wild elephants. The keeper fancied he saw his long-lost elephant in a group that was before them. He was determined to go up to it, nor could the strongest representations of the great danger dissuade him from his purpose. When he approached the creature, she knew him, and giving him three salutes by waving her trunk in the air, knelt down and received him on her back. She afterwards assisted in securing the other elephants, and likewise brought with her three young ones, which she had produced during her absence. The keeper recovered his character, and, as a recompense for his sufferings and intrepidity, had

an annuity settled on him for life. This elephant was afterwards in the possession of Governor Hastings.

138. A small body of sepoys stationed at an outpost —Fort de Galle, in Ceylon—to protect a granary containing a large quantity of rice, was suddenly removed, in order to quiet some unruly villagers, a few miles distant, who had set our authorities at defiance. Two of our party happened to be on the spot at the moment. No sooner had the sepoys withdrawn, than a herd of wild elephants, which had been long noticed in the neighbourhood, made their appearance in front of the granary. They had been preceded by a scout, which returned to the herd, and having no doubt satisfied them in a language which to them needed no interpreter that the coast was clear, they advanced at a brisk pace towards the building. When they arrived within a few yards of it, quite in martial order, they made a sudden stand, and began deliberately to reconnoitre the object of their attack. Nothing could be more wary and methodical than their proceedings. The walls of the granary were of solid brickwork, very thick, and the only opening into the building was in the centre of the terraced roof, to which the ascent was by a ladder. On the approach of the elephants, the two astonished spectators clambered up into a lofty banyan tree, in order to escape mischief. The conduct of the four-footed besiegers was such as strongly to excite their curiosity, and they therefore watched their proceedings with intense anxiety. The two spectators were so completely screened by the foliage of the tree to which they had resorted for safety, that they could

not be perceived by the elephants, though they could
see very well through the little vistas formed by the
separated branches what was going on below. Had
there been a door to the granary, all difficulty of
obtaining an entrance would have instantly vanished;
but four thick brick walls were obstacles which seemed
at once to defy both the strength and sagacity of these
dumb robbers. Nothing daunted by the magnitude of
the difficulty which they had to surmount, they successively began their operations at the angles of the
building. A large male elephant, with tusks of immense
proportions, laboured for some time to make an impression; but after a while, his strength was exhausted,
and he retired. The next in size and strength then
advanced, and exhausted his exertions, with no better
success. A third then came forward, and applying
those tremendous levers with which his jaws were
armed, and which he wielded with such prodigious
might, he at length succeeded in dislodging a brick.
An opening once made, other elephants advanced, when
an entrance was soon obtained, sufficiently large to
admit the determined marauders. As the whole herd
could not be accommodated at once, they divided into
small bodies of three or four. One of them entered,
and when they had taken their fill, they retired, and
their places were immediately supplied by the next in
waiting, until the whole herd, upwards of twenty, had
made a full meal. By this time a shrill sound was
heard from one of the elephants, which was readily
understood, when those that were still in the building
immediately rushed out, and joined their companions.

One of the first division, after retiring from the granary, had acted as sentinel while the rest were enjoying the fruits of their sagacity and perseverence. He had so stationed himself as to be enabled to observe the advance of an enemy from any quarter, and upon perceiving the troops as they returned from the village, he sounded the signal of retreat, when the whole herd, flourishing their trunks, moved rapidly into the jungle The soldiers, on their return, found that the animals had devoured the greater part of the rice. A ball from a field-piece was discharged at them in their retreat ; but they only wagged their tails, as if in mockery, and soon disappeared in the recesses of their native forests.

139. In general, the elephant makes less use of his strength than his address, often applying the most dexterous methods of accomplishing his ends. I was one day, says Mr Jesse, feeding the poor elephant at Exeter 'Change with potatoes, which he took out of my hand. One of them, a round one, fell on the floor, just out of the reach of his proboscis. He leaned against his wooden bar, put out his trunk, and could just touch the potato, but could not pick it up. After several ineffectual efforts, he at last blew the potato against the opposite wall with sufficient force to make it rebound, and he then without difficulty secured it.

140. M. Phillipe, quoted by Buffon, was an eye witness to the following equally wonderful facts :—He one day went to the river at Goa, near to which place a large ship was building, and where an area was filled with beams and planks for the purpose. Some men tied the

ends of heavy beams with a rope, which was handed to
an elephant, who carried it to his mouth, and after
twisting it round his trunk, drew it, without any con-
ductor, to the place where the ship was building. One
of the animals sometimes drew beams so large, that
more than twenty men would have been necessary to
move. But what surprised M. Phillipe most was, that
when other beams obstructed the road, this elephant
raised the ends of his own beam, or edged it forward,
as the case might be, that it might clear those which
lay in his way. Could the most enlightened man have
done more?

141. At Mahè, on the coast of Malabar, M. Toreesa
tells us he had an opportunity of admiring the sagacity of
an elephant displayed in a similar manner. Its master
had let it for a certain sum per day, and its employment
was to carry with its trunk timber for a building out of
the river. This busine'ss it despatched very dexterously,
under the command of a boy; and afterwards laid the
pieces one upon another in such exact order, that no
man could have done it better.

142. To give an idea of these labours, it is sufficient
to remark, that all the tuns, sacks, and bales transported
from one place to another in India, are carried by
elephants; that they carry burdens on their bodies,
their necks, their tusks, and even in their mouths, by
giving them the end of a rope, which they hold fast
with their teeth; that uniting sagacity to strength, they
never break or injure anything committed to their
charge; that from the banks of the rivers they put
these bundles into boats, without wetting them, laying

2 K

them down gently, and arranging them where they
ought to be placed; that when deposited in the places
where their masters direct, they try with their trunks
whether the goods are properly stowed; and if a tun or
cask rolls, they go of their own accord in quest of
stones to prop and render it firm.

143. It is remarked by Terry, in his voyage to the East
Indies, that the elephant performs many actions which
would seem almost the effect of human reason. He
does everything his master commands. If he is directed
to terrify any person, he runs upon him with every
appearance of fury, and when he comes near, stops
short without doing him the least injury. When the
master chooses to affront any one, he tells the elephant,
who collects water and mud with his trunk, and squirts
it upon the object pointed out to him.

144. At the siege of Bhurtpore, in the year 1805, an
affair occurred between two elephants, which displays
at once the character and mental capability, the passions,
cunning, and resources of these curious animals. The
British army, with its countless host of followers and
attendants, and thousands of cattle, had been for a
long time before the city, when, on the approach of the
hot season and of the dry hot winds, the water in the
neighbourhood of the camps necessary for the supply
of so many beings began to fail; the ponds or tanks
had dried up, and no more water was left than the
immense wells of the country would furnish. The
multitude of men and cattle that were unceasingly at
the wells, particularly the largest, occasioned no little
struggle for the priority in procuring the supply for

which each was there to seek, and the consequent confusion on the spot was frequently very considerable.
On one occasion, two elephant-drivers, each with his
elephant, the one remarkably large and strong, and the
other comparatively small and weak, were at the well
together; the small elephant had been provided by his
master with a bucket for the occasion, which he carried
at the end of his proboscis; but the larger animal
being destitute of this necessary vessel, either sponta-
neously, or by desire of his keeper, seized the bucket,
and easily wrested it from his less powerful fellow-ser-
vant. The latter was too sensible of his inferiority
openly to resent the insult, though it is obvious that he
felt it, but great squabbling and abuse ensued between
the keepers. At length the weaker animal, watching
the opportunity when the other was standing with his
side to the well, retired backwards a few paces in a very
quiet unsuspicious manner, and then rushing forward
with all his might, drove his head against the side of
the other, and fairly pushed him into the well. It may
easily be imagined that great inconvenience was immediately experienced, and serious apprehensions quickly
followed that the water in the well, on which the
existence of so many seemed in a great measure to
depend, would be spoiled, or at least injured, by the
unwieldy brute thus precipitated into it; and as the
surface of the water was nearly twenty feet below the
common level, there did not appear to be any means
that could be adopted to get the animal out by main
force, at least without injuring him. There were many
feet of water below the elephant, who floated with ease

on its surface, and experiencing considerable pleasure
from his cool retreat, evinced but little inclination even
to exert what means he might possess in himself of
escape. A vast number of fascines had been employed
by the army in conducting the siege, and at length it
occurred to the elephant-keeper that a sufficient number
of these (which may be compared to bundles of wood)
might be lowered into the well to make a pile, which
might be raised to the top, if the animal could be
instructed as to the necessary means of laying them in
regular succession under his feet. Permission having
been obtained from the engineer officers to use the
fascines, which were at the time put away in several
piles of very considerable height, the keeper had to
teach the elephant the lesson which, by means of that
extraordinary ascendency these men attain over the
elephants, joined with the intellectual resources of the
animal itself, he was soon enabled to do, and the elephant began quickly to place each fascine, as it was
lowered to him, successively under him, until in a little
time he was enabled to stand upon them. By this time,
however, the cunning brute, enjoying the pleasure of
his situation, after the heat and partial privation of
water to which he had been lately exposed, (they are
observed in their natural state to frequent rivers, and
to swim very often), was unwilling to work any longer,
and all the threats of his keeper could not induce him
to place another fascine. The man then opposed
cunning to cunning, and began to caress and praise the
elephant, and what he could not effect by threats, he
was enabled to do by the repeated promise of plenty of

rack. Incited by this, the animal again went to work, raised himself considerably higher, until, by a partial removal of the masonry round the top of the well, he was enabled to step out. The whole affair occupied about fourteen hours.

145. The elephant manifests also a most marvellous instinct in relation to the great weight of his body. He seems to have a kind of knowledge that his ponderous mass is of unusual and extraordinary heaviness, for when he is required to pass over an unsafe bridge, or other artificial road, he suspects the danger with wonderful prescience, although man is unable to detect any defect in the structure. In one of the Indian expeditions, an artificial road, formed by the trunks of trees, was made on a difficult ascent, up which it was designed each elephant should drag a gun. Having cut a good deal of the most prominent part of the hill away, and laid trees on the ascent as a footing for the elephants, these animals were made to approach it, which the first did with some reluctance and fear. He looked up, shook his head, and when forced by his driver, roared piteously. There can be no question, in my opinion, that this sagacious animal was competent instinctively to judge of the practicability of the artificial flight of steps thus constructed, for the moment some little alteration was made, he then seemed willing to approach. He commenced his examination and scrutiny by pressing with his trunk the trees that had been thrown across, and after this he put his fore leg on with great caution, raising the fore part of his body so as to throw its weight on the tree. This done he

seemed satisfied as to its stability. The next step for
him to ascend by was a projecting rock, which we could
not remove. The same sagacious examinations took
place, the elephant keeping his flat side close to the
bank, and leaning against it. The next step was against
a tree; but this, on the first pressure of his trunk, he
did not like. Force was at length resorted to, and the
elephant roared terrifically, but would not move; something was then removed, he seemed satisfied as before,
and he ascended that stupendous ghaut.

146. The female elephant, only seven years old, that
was taken to the Adelphi, to repeat some parts she
had performed in Paris, likewise carefully ascertained
the safety of the stage before she ventured her whole
weight upon it.

147. There is another habit of elephants which is
proper to our subject, and which, therefore, we shall
just notice. It is the understanding they have, or the
arrangement they make, when a whole herd, amounting
sometimes to 300, is on its march to open a new track
through a dense forest of trees. The large male elephants always put themselves in the van, and proceed
in some cases to tear down the branches, and in others
to uproot the trees which obstruct the passage, that a
way may be cleared for the females, and those of youth
and weakness, which follow in the wake in single file.
How do all come to this mutual understanding? How
do the tall and strong individuals know that it becomes
them to undertake the most difficult task in the operation? Do they assume it instinctively, and the others
instinctively assent to it? or is the arrangement come

to by appointment? The secret no doubt lies in an instinct.

14⁸. There are so many anecdotes of this animal's execution of the most rigid justice, by making the culprit feel the weight of his vengeance, and so many instances of his sagacity likewise put upon record in almost all books of natural history, that it is unnecessary to introduce any here; nor, were we so inclined, would our space admit of it. But one instance of the latter, most nobly displayed, shall have a place. The favourite elephant of the grand vizier under Rajah Dowlah was the hero of the noble feat. This great nabob was about to make the diversion of a mighty hunt in the neighbourhood of Lucknow, where the game was rather plentiful. The preparations being complete, and a train of Indian nobility assembled, the procession of Nimrods began to move off for the field. After passing through a ravine, the gorgeous sportsmen entered a meadow, which was covered with sick people who were lying exposed to get the benefit of the pure and fresh air, and they were so distributed as to obstruct the course of the beasts of burden. Rajah Dowlah was intent upon feasting his cruel eyes with the sight that the mangling of the bodies of the miserable creatures would produce, by compelling the huge elephants to trample them under-foot. The grand vizier rode upon his own beast, and the nabob ordered the driver to goad him on, and he went at a quick pace; but when he arrived at the spot of the indisposed people, though in a trot, the sagacious animal stopt short before the first invalid. The vizier cursed him, the driver goaded him, and the nabob cried, " Stick him in the ear!" All, however, was vain. More humane than his superiors, the elephant stood firm and refused to violate his better feelings  At length, seeing the poor creatures helpless and unable to move themselves out of his way, he took up the first with his trunk and laid him gently down again out of his path. He did the same with the second, and third, and so on, until he had made a clear passage, along which the retinue could pass without doing injury to any of them. The brute and the man had made an exchange of their proper sentiments, and humanity triumphed gloriously in the animal. We question whether another instance of such strong and humane sagacity can be produced from any region in the animal kingdom.

140. According to Ælian, the elephants of Germanicus were trained to take part in the performances of the Roman theatre. There, among the assembled thousands, they appeared quite at home, lost all dread of the clashing of cymbals, and moved in cadence to the sounds of the notes of the flute. Upon one occasion when a particular exhibition of the docility of these elephants was required, twelve of the most sagacious and well-trained were selected, who, marching into the theatre with a regular step, at the voice of the keeper, moved in harmonious measure, sometimes in a circle, and sometimes divided into parties, scattering flowers over the pavement. In the intervals of the dance, they would beat time to the music, still preserving their proper order. The Romans, with their accustomed luxury, feasted the elephants, after this

display, with prodigal magnificence. Splendid couches were placed in the arena, ornamented with paintings, and covered with tapestry. Before the couches, upon tables of ivory and cedar, was spread the banquet of the elephants, in vessels of gold and silver. The preparations being completed, the twelve elephants marched in, six males clad in robes of men, and six females attired as women. They lay down in order upon their couches, or ' *tricliniums* of festival recumbency,' and, at a signal, extended their trunks and ate with most praise-worthy moderation. Not one of them, says Ælian, appeared the least voracious, or manifested any disposition for an unequal share of the food, or an undue proportion of the delicacies. They were as moderate also in their drink, and received the cups which were presented to them with the greatest decorum. According to Pliny, at the spectacles given by Germinicus, it was not an uncommon thing to see elephants hurl javelins in the air, and catch them in their trunks, fight with each other as gladiators, and then execute a Pyrrhic dance. Lastly, they danced upon a rope, and their steps were so practised and certain, that four of them traversed the rope, or rather parallel ropes, bearing a litter which contained one of their companions, who feigned to be sick This feat of dancing or walking upon a rope might perhaps be doubted, if it rested merely upon the testimony of a single author; but the practice is confirmed by many ancient writers of authority, who agree with Pliny that the elephants trained at Rome would not only walk along a rope forward, but retire backward with equal precision.

150. Sonnini mentions an elephant at Naples, which
was employed with others in fetching water in a copper
vessel, and perceiving that the water escaped from some
fracture, he took the vessel of his own accord to a
smith's for repair, in imitation of what he had seen
done before by his master.

151. The elephant. docile as he is, a noble quadruped,
seems conscious of his superiority over the rest of the
brute creation. A proof of this may be seen in the
following circumstance related by an eastern tourist.
Some young camels were travelling with the British
army in India, when, having occasion to cross the
Jumna in a boat, and the driver being unable to urge
them forward, the elephant was appealed to to accom-
plish the task; the animal immediately assumed a
furious appearance, trumpeted with his proboscis, shook
his ears, roared, struck the ground right and left, and
blew the dust in clouds towards them. The camels, in
their fear of the elephant, forgot their dread of the
boat, and they rushed into it in the greatest hurry,
when the elephant resumed his composure, and deliberately returned to his post.

152. The elephant, unwieldy and uncouth as he
seems, presents some remarkable features of character,
combining the fidelity of the dog, the endurance of the
camel, and the docility of the horse, with singular
sagacity, prudence, and courage. It is related of one
of the soldiers of Pyrrhus, King of Epirus, that, when
fighting in the territory of Argos, he fell wounded from
his elephant, which, rushing furiously among the combatants till he found his master, raised him gently from

the ground with his trunk, and placing him on his tusks, carried him back to the town. A similar anecdote is given of King Porus, who, in an engagement with Alexander the Great, meeting with a similar casualty, his faithful elephant is said to have kept the enemy at bay till he had replaced the monarch on his back by means of his trunk, although the poor animal, in this heroic defence, was severely wounded.

153. In one of the recent accounts of scenes of Indian warfare, a body of artillery was described as proceeding up a hill, and the great strength of elephants was found highly advantageous in drawing up the guns. On the carriage of one of these guns, a little in front of the wheel, sat an artilleryman, resting himself. An elephant drawing another gun was advancing in regular order close behind; whether from falling asleep, or over fatigue, the man fell from his seat, and the wheel of the gun-carriage, with a heavy gun, was just rolling over him. The elephant comprehending the danger, and seeing that he could not reach the body of the man with his trunk, seized the wheel by the top, and lifted it up, passed it carefully over the fallen man, and set it down on the other side.

154. Take another example of the shrewd wit of this colossal creature. Some men were teasing an elephant they were conveying across a river. In the boat that was towed along-side they had a dog which began to torment it by pulling its ears. The elephant was resolved to resent the impertinence, and what do you suppose was her expedient? She filled her proboscis with water, and then deluged the whole party. At first

the men laughed at the manœuvre, but she persisted until they were compelled to bale, to keep from sinking. Seeing this, she redoubled her efforts ; and, it is said, she certainly would have swamped the boat, had the passage across been prolonged a few minutes further. Thus much—although much more might be presented —in behalf of the noble qualities of the elephant. We see that he is in no respect inferior to the dog in character; and yet, since the most excellent things are said to lie in a small compass, and the dog does not, like his monstrous contemporary, require two hundred pounds of solid food per diem, or take up so much room,—the prevailing preference for the canine animal will doubtless long continue to obtain among civilized communities.

# THE MONKEY.

—••‡‡••—

He prayeth best, who loveth best
All things both great and small;
For the dear GOD who loveth us,
He made and loveth all.—COLERIDGE.

155. AN officer dining at our mess over-heard a conversation concerning monkeys, and some one said that
if a man had once shot at and wounded a monkey, he
would be a hard-hearted heathen indeed if he repeated
the act, as its cries, actions, and especially the way it
moved its hands about the wounded part were very
piteous, and almost human-like. Yes, said our guest,
monkeys are singular creatures. I was out shooting
to-day, and saw a troop in a grove of trees. As I had
a bullet in my gun I fired and killed one. He fell from
the branch to the ground, and the others made such a
chattering and played such antics, that I hid behind
a tree to watch them. Presently one old grey-headed
fellow came down the tree, looked suspiciously at the
body, touched it, turned it over, and finding it quite
dead, commenced howling till all the monkeys drew
round him. After chattering for some time, they all
withdrew a little distance with the exception of thirteen,
one of whom, seemingly a person of authority, sat in
the centre, the remainder forming a circle round him.

L

They first examined the body, and after jabbering amongst themselves some time, the old grey-beard came forward, touched the body, and chattered, apparently detailing the finding of the body. Others then came forward, and pointed to the spot where I stood when I fired. and seemed by their pantomimes to detail the manner by which their unfortunate brother had come to his death After several witnesses had been examin ed, the thirteen consulted, and shortly after left, and the other monkeys came down and removed the body and all quitted the place.

156 In a family where a common monkey was a pet, on one occasion. the footman had been shaving himself the monkey watching him during the process, when he carelessly left his apparatus within reach of th creature. As soon as the man was gone out of the room, the monkey got the razor and began to scrape away at his throat as he had seen the footman do; when, alas! not understanding the nature of the instrument he was using. the animal cut its own throat and before it was discovered bled to death.

157. In the countries of the eastern Peninsula and Archipelago, where they abound, the matrons are often observed, in the cool of the evening. sitting in a circle round their little ones, which amuse themselves with various gambols. The merriment of the young, as they jump over each others heads. make mimic fights, and wrestle in sport, is most ludicrously contrasted with the gravity of their seniors, who might be presumed to be delighting in the fun, but far too staid and wise to let it appear. There is a regard however to discipline;

and whenever any foolish juvenile behaves decidedly ill, the mamma will be seen to jump into the throng, sieze the offender by the tail, and administer exactly that extreme kind of chastisement which has so long been in vogue among human parents and Yorkshire school-masters.

158. A monkey tied to a stake was robbed by the Johnny Crows (in the West Indies) of his food, and he conceived the following plan of punishing the thieves. He feigned death, and lay perfectly motionless on the ground, near to his stake. The birds approached by degrees, and got near enough to steal his food, which he allowed them to do. This he repeated several times, till they became so bold as to come within the reach of his claws. He calculated his distance, and laid hold of one of them. Death was not his plan of punishment, he was more refined in his cruelty. He plucked every feather out of the bird. and then let him go and show himself to his companions. He made a man of him, according to the ancient definition of a "biped without feathers."

159. Rajah Brooke, of Sarawak, narrates an interest-ing tale of a'female ourang-outang, which when severely wounded, ceased her attempts to escape, and weaving together a branch platform, seated herself upon it, and quietly awaited her end. The poor animal received several more shots before she expired, and as she fell dead upon her temporary edifice, the hunters were put to some trouble before they could dislodge the dead body. The whole process of weaving the branches and seating herself did not occupy more than a minute.

160. Dr. Guthrie tells the following amusing anecdote of a reasonable monkey. Jack, as he was called, seeing his master and some companions drinking—with those imitative powers for which his species is remarkable, finding half a glass of whiskey left, took it up and drank it off. It flew, of course, to his head. Amid their loud roars of laughter he began to skip, hop, and dance. Jack was drunk. Next day, when they went with the intention of repeating the fun, to take the poor monkey from his box, he was not to be seen. Looking inside, there he lay, crouching in a corner. " Come out!" said his master. Afraid to disobey, he came walking on three legs ; the fore paw, that was laid on his forehead, saying, as plain as words could do, that he had a headache. Having left him some days to get well and resume his gaiety, they at length carried him off to the old scene of revel. On entering, he eyed the glasses with manifest terror, skulking behind the chair ; and on his master ordering him to drink, he was on the house top in a twinkling. They called him down. He would not come. His master shook the whip at him. Jack, astride on the ridge-pole, grinned defiance. A gun, of which he was always much afraid, was pointed at this disciple of temperance ; he ducked his head, and slipped over to the back of the house ; upon which, seeing his predicament, and less afraid apparently of the fire than the fire-water, the monkey leaped at a bound on the chimney top, and getting down into a flue, held on by his fore paws. He would rather be singed than drunk. He triumphed, and although his master kept him for twelve years

after that, he never could persuade the monkey to taste another drop of whiskey.

161. All the apes of this genus possess large powers of imitation; and their propensity to indulge in such often betrays them into trouble, which sometimes terminates in capture, sometimes in death. Ever watchful and attentive to all the actions of man, they descend from their posts of observation, and then endeavour to imitate, as near as possible, all they have seen performed. The ape catchers take advantage of this propensity, and, in some instances, place a vessel of water in a situation that is open to the view of the animals perched upon the trees. The men take care to dabble well in the vessel, and to wash their hands, particularly their faces with a great deal of attention, that they may set a copy worthy of the brute's ambition to do the like. All this being done, the water is poured out, and its place supplied with a solution of glue. The article is left for the inspection of the meddling mimics, who never fail, unless they have been previously caught, to handle and apply it in the manner their entrappers were observed to handle and apply the water. Unwarily, they set to in good earnest, bedaubing their faces with the treacherous liquid, and soon their eyelids become glued over the sockets, and being thus blindfolded, they cannot effect escape for want of sight, and they then present an easy prey to their captors.

162. Another mode of ensnaring them is by means of intoxicating drinks. The apes being known to be fond of spirituous liquors, the person who wishes to

2 L

# THE MONKEY.

163. It is said that the Indians sometimes direct
leave the work to be performed by the animals at will.
These creatures seeing a heap or two commenced,

164. ——" They are coming towards the bridge; they
Raoul. " How? swim it," I asked, " it is a torrent
leap the stream, they will bridge it." " Bridge it ! and
how ? " " Stop a moment captain, you shall see." The

like so many soldiers. They were, as Raoul had stated, of the comadreja or ring-tailed tribe. One, an aide-de-camp or chief pioneer perhaps, ran out upon a projecting rock, and appeared to communicate with the leader. This produced a movement in the troop. Commands were issued, and fatigue parties were detached, and marched to the front. Meanwhile, several of the comadrejas—engineers, no doubt—ran along the bank, examining the trees on both sides of the *arroyo*. At length they all collected round a tall cotton-wood tree that grew over the narrowest part of the stream, and twenty or thirty of them scampered up its trunk. On reaching a high point, the foremost, a strong fellow, ran out upon a limb, and taking several turns of his tail around it, slipped off, and hung head downwards. The next on the limb, also a stout one, climbed down the body of the first, and whipping his tail tightly round the neck and fore-arm of the latter, dropped off in his turn, and hung head down. The third repeated this manœuvre upon the second, and the fourth upon the third, and so on, until the last upon the string rested his fore-paws on the ground. The living chain now commenced swinging backwards and forwards, like the pendulum of a clock. The motion was slight at first, but gradually increased, the lowermost monkey striking his hands violently on the earth as he passed the tangent of the oscillating curve. Several others upon the limbs above aided the movement. This continued until the monkey at the end of the chain was thrown among the branches of a tree on the opposite bank. Here, after two or three vibrations,

he clutched a limb, and held fast. This movement
was executed adroitly, just at the culminating point of
the oscillation, in order to save the immediate links
from the violence of a too sudden jerk. The chain
was now fast at both ends, forming a complete suspension bridge, over which the whole troop, to the number
of four or five hundred, passed with the rapidity of
thought. It was one of the most comical sights I ever
beheld, to witness the quizzical expression of countenances along that living chain. The troop was now on
the other side, but how were the animals forming the
bridge to get themselves over? This was the question
that suggested itself. Manifestly, by number one
letting go his tail. But then the *point d'appui* on the
other side was much lower down, and number one with
half a dozen of his neighbours, would be dashed
against the opposite bank, or soused into the water.
Here then, was a problem; and we waited with some
curiosity for its solution. It was soon solved. A
monkey was now seen attaching his tail to the lowest
on the bridge, another girdled him in a similar manner,
and another, and so on, until a dozen more were added
to the string. These last were all powerful fellows;
and running up to a high limb, they lifted the bridge
into a position almost horizontal. Then a scream from
the last monkey of the new formation warned the tail
end that all was ready, and the next moment the whole
chain was swung over, and landed safely on the
opposite bank. The lowermost links now dropped
off like a melting candle, whilst the higher ones leaped
to the branches and came down by the trunk. The

whole troop then scampered off into the chapparal,
and disappeared.

165. M. de Maisonpré was once a witness of a single
male ape, of a larger species, finding his way within
the walls surrounding the pagoda of Cheringham,
which enclosed a district claimed by the community
of a smaller species ; for, it appears, that certain herds
of them live together in this way, and assert their
rights to the possession of particular provinces, and,
if necessary, will take up arms to defend them. The
trespasser was very quickly made to understand that
he had got into an enemy's country. The alarm cry
being given, numbers of the resident males put themselves in a posture of attack. Though the interloper
was much larger and stronger than any of his assailants, he yet seemed to be aware that the contest would
be unequal on a fair field, for he betook himself to a
stratagem, and fled for an advantageous position on
the top of the pagoda, which was eleven stories in
height; and when faced about on the pinnacle of it, he
saw a number of his enemies in force at his heels.
His sagacity and generalship now proved the means
of his safety. Being himself secure upon a narrow
dome, he, taking advantage of his superior personal
strength, instantly seized four of his furious pursuers,
and as furiously hurled them down from the dizzy top.
This was sufficient to warn and intimidate the rest;
and after a great deal of noisy clamour, they resolved
on a retreat, which they effected in safety, leaving the
intruder unavenged upon his perch. Here he took

care to remain till the evening, when he was able to get clear off.

166. A hundred and fifty years ago a chimpanzee was brought into England, which had been caught in Angola, far up the country. It was a male, and at the time of its capture had a female in company. It was soon rendered tame, and became an exceedingly gentle creature. The persons he knew on board the vessel he was accustomed to embrace with apparently great tenderness. There were several monkeys in the ship, but on no occasion would he associate with them. In many of his actions, he displayed great sagacity. A suit of clothes was made for him, in the wearing of which, after a little time, he took great delight. Any part of his attire which he could not put on by himself he would bring in his paws to any one of the ship's company for assistance. He would lie down at night in a bed allotted to him, place his head calmly on the pillow, and carefully pull up the bed clothes, in order to secure their full warmth. He did not long survive his arrival in London.

167. A female chimpanzee was procured by Captain Payne in the Isle of Princes, in the Gulf of Guinea, from a native trader who had carried it thither from the banks of the Gaboon. It was a young animal, and far inferior in size to specimens often seen in the recesses of its native forests. There, it is said, this species attains the height of five or six feet; it is a formidable antagonist to the elephant, and several of them will not scruple to attack the lion and other beasts of prey with clubs. The negroes generally believe that the chim-

panzee is rational, and even can speak, but cunningly
avoids doing so lest it should be compelled to labour.
When this animal came on board it shook hands with
some of the sailors, but refused its hand angrily to
others, without any apparent cause. It speedily, however, became familiar with the crew, except one boy, to
whom it was never reconciled. When the seamen's
mess was brought on deck it was a constant attendant;
it would go round and embrace each person, while it
uttered loud yells, and would then seat itself among
them to share the repast: when angry, it sometimes
made a barking noise like a dog; at other times it
would cry like a pettish child, and scratch itself with
great vehemence. It expressed pleasure, especially on
receiving sweetmeats, by a sound like a "hem," in a
grave tone, but it seemed to have little variety of voice.
At that time it had no relish for wine, but afterwards
seemed to like it; but it never could endure ardent
spirits. It once stole a bottle of wine, which it uncorked
with its teeth and began to drink. It liked coffee, and
was immoderately fond of whatever was sweet. It
learned to feed itself with a spoon, to drink out of a
glass, and was generally disposed to imitate all the
actions of man which it observed. It was attracted by
bright metals, seemed to take a pride in clothes, and
often placed a cocked hat on its head. It appeared a
timid creature, and was particularly afraid of fire arms.
It lived with Captain Payne for seventeen weeks, two of
which were spent in Cork and Liverpool. In the latter
town it languished for a few days, moaned heavily,

became oppressed in its breathing, and died with con-
vulsive motions of its limbs.

168. A female chimpanzee on board a vessel manifested great intelligence. She had been taught to heat
the oven, and take care that no coals should fall out.
She knew well when the temperature was adapted to
baking, and never failed to fetch the baker, who implicitly trusted to her, in good time. She also assisted in
unfurling the sails, splicing the ropes, and could even
row along with the sailors. The vessel in which she
was seen was bound for America, but she did not live
to reach it in consequence of an act of great cruelty.
On one occasion the mate inflicted a very severe punishment upon her, which she did not deserve. and which
she bore with the utmost fortitude, only holding out
her hands to break the force of the blows, and at the
same time entreating for mercy. But from that time
she refused all sustenance, and died from grief and
hunger on the fifth day, lamented by all on board
except the unfeeling mate.

169. According to M. D'Obsonville, the female apes
manifest a considerable degree of tenderness towards
their offspring; and what is very remarkable, they
exercise, sometimes at least, their parental authority in
a sort of judicial and strictly impartial form. The
young ones were seen to sport and gambol with one
another in the presence of their mother, who sat ready
to give judgment and punish misdemeanours, when any
one was found guilty of foul play or malicious conduct
towards another of the family, the parent interfered by
seizing the young criminal by the tail, which she held

fast with one of her paws, till she boxed its ears with the other. Now we do not know of anything exactly similar to this in any other tribe of animals. The proper performance of such an act most certainly implies a very considerable amount of understanding. There is another habit, too, peculiar to these creatures, that if true, requires no less intelligence than the one just named. It is said that when any one of them receives a wound with an arrow, the whole community fly to its assistance, but instead of pulling out the missile, which by so doing would lacerate the flesh and give pain, they bite off the shaft only, and thus allow the unfortunate animal to go away with the remainder in its body. It is also affirmed of the baboons that they will nip off the sting of a scorpion with so much dexterity and rapidity, that they leave no time for the venomous weapon to produce any effect upon their hands, and that being done, the apes devour the scorpions with much greediness. The natives dread them, for they will plunder their villages, rob their orchards, and retire leisurely with the booty. Sometimes they appear to do the latter business by method. A sentinel is appointed to watch, while a part of the company enter the enclosure, and a part remain without; the latter form a line to the place of depôt and the former gather the fruit. If the wall is high, a small force takes station upon it, and these, after receiving the produce from those within, throw it to those in a line without. It is then passed along the line to its hiding-place, which is generally in some crag of a mountain.

170. As an instance of the monkey's apparent gravity, even in the midst of frolic, Mrs. Lee tells an amusing story of some pigs that were allowed to run about the deck occasionally, and Jack would then sometimes suddenly spring on the back of one of them, his face to the tail, and away scampered his frightened steed. Sometimes an obstacle would impede the gallop, and then Jack, loosening the hold which he had acquired by digging his nails into the skin of the pig, industriously tried to uncurl its tail, and if he were saluted by a laugh from some one near by, he would look up with an assumed air of wonder, as much as to say, " What can you find to laugh at ?"

171. The same authoress informs us of another in the Jardin des Plantes, in Paris, that she very much annoyed by striking him on his paws for some misbehaviour towards one of his companions, and the monkey seemed ever afterwards to recollect this treatment, when, at least, this associating power of her presence came to the aid of his memory, for on future occasions, he no sooner saw her, or heard her voice, than he threw himself into a passion, rolled about in rage, and in one instance seized her gown, and dragged a portion of it within the bars of his cage, when he then tore a piece out of it, although it was made of some stout material.

172. The case of the Barbary ape and the preacher Casauban, related by Mrs. Louden, is perhaps an instance of imitation as ludicrous as anything of the kind that has ever been witnessed. Father Casauban brought up the animal in question, and having become

attached to him, it wished to follow him wherever he
went. One day when Casauban was going to church,
the ape, not being made secure, followed its master to
the place of worship, and being a good climber, silently
mounted the sounding board, and there lay quiet and
concealed till the sermon was in course of delivery.
It then advanced to the edge of its perch to see what
was going on beneath it, and to watch the actions of
the orator. These were no sooner observed by the
able mimic, than it began to perform also, and its
imitation of the preacher's gestures were so perfectly
grotesque, that the whole congregation was put into a
state of great risibility, and such that could not be
suppressed. The good father was alike shocked, and
indignant at the ill-timed levity of his audience, and
began to minister some severe reproofs. But. seeing
all his efforts failing, he launched forth into violent
action, accompanied by loud vociferations. His
frequent gestures the ape did not fail to take up
immediately, with no less animation than that which
inspirited his master. And at this apparent competi-
tion of the two individuals, the people burst into roars
of laughter; and when the animal was pointed out to
the pastor, though highly exasperated, it is said that
he could scarcely command his own countenance
while he gave directions to have the ape removed.

173. In 1776, one being conveyed to Holland, was
observed, when about to lie down on board at the
approach of night, to prepare her bed, by shaking well
the hay on which she slept, and, after putting it in
proper order, would wrap herself snugly up in the

quilt. In addition to the making of her bed very
neatly every day, M. le Guat saw one at Java that was
accustomed to bind up her head with a handkerchief
before she retired to rest. The former, on the voyage
to Holland, noticed that the padlock of her chain was
opened with a key. The ape soon began to practise
the manœuvre by taking up a little bit of stick, and
after putting it in the key-hole of the lock, endeavoured to open it by turning the stick in all directions.
One morning when on shore, she escaped from her
chair, and it was then when the real and beautiful
instinct of the animal displayed itself. This was from
the immediate impulse to climb, and accordingly she
was seen ascending with surprising agility the beams
and oblique rafters of a building. Being endowed,
like all the species, with extraordinary strength, and
capable of prodigious celerity, she was not retaken
without some considerable trouble. Though but two
feet and a half high, she was nearly a match for the
combined strength of four men, who found it necessary
to put forth all their efforts in order to secure her.
This they effected by two of them seizing her legs,
while a third took charge of her head, and the other
fastened a collar round her neck. It is no wonder
then that the full grown ourang of seven or eight feet
in height, should prove a formidable adversary to the
united force of ten men. During the time of her
liberty, she took the cork from a bottle of Malaga
wine, and appeared highly gratified with the contents,
which she drank to the very last drop, and then put
the bottle in its place again

174. A friend of our's possessed one of these creatures, whose disposition seemed very affectionate; if it had done wrong and was scolded, it immediately seated itself on the floor, and clasping its hands together seemed to beg earnestly to be forgiven.

175. Mrs. Lee mentions of the monkey on board the vessel with herself, that Jack, for such was his name, would sometimes scald or burn his fingers, by snatching out the herbs from the hot beverage; the pain would keep him quiet for a few days, but no sooner had it been alleviated, than Jack repeated his tricks, and again suffered the penalty. Was this owing to any absence of memory in the monkey, or did he, like mankind, too often commit the deed right in the face of the consequence? No doubt that man does this injustice to himself much more often than does any brute whatever. He will gratify some appetite for a moment, although he knows full well that the pain which will certainly follow will be neither light nor short. The probability is, that Jack's knowledge of the past ceased with the pain; at least we should judge so from analogy, because those animals which appear to have a memory active when assisted by the power of association, are not found to be so easily taken in when that is present. This kind of memory although exceedingly imperfect, is nevertheless sufficient to enable them to profit by experience.

176. Of a monkey which a man in Paris had trained to a variety of clever tricks, the same writer gives an interesting account. I met him one day says he, suddenly as he was coming up the drawing-room stairs. He

M

made way for me by standing in an angle, and when I
said, 'Good morning', took off his cap, and made me a
low bow. 'Are you going away?' I asked; 'where is
your passport?' Upon which he took from the same
cap a square piece of paper, which he opened and showed to me. His master told him my gown was dusty,
and he instantly took a small brush from his master's
pocket, raised the hem of my dress, cleaned it, and then
did the same for my shoes. He was perfectly docile
and obedient; when we gave him something to eat, he
did not cram his pouches with it, but delicately and
tidily devoured it, and when we bestowed money on
him, he immediately put it into his master's hands.

177. I have frequently, says Margrave, speaking of
another species, been a witness of their assemblies and
deliberations. Every day, both morning and evening,
the Ouarines assemble in the woods to receive instructions. When all come together, one among the number
takes the highest place on a tree, and makes a signal
with his hand to the rest to sit round, in order to hearken.
As soon as he sees them placed, he begins his discourse
with so loud a voice, and yet in a manner so precipitate,
that to hear him at a distance, one would think the
whole company were crying out at the same time;
however, during that time, one only is speaking, and all
the rest observe the most profound silence. When this
is done, he makes a sign with the hand for the rest to
reply, and at that instant they raise their voices together,
until by another signal of the hand they are enjoined
silence. This they as readily obey, till at last the whole

assembly break up after hearing a repetition of the same preachment.

178. Le Vaillant, when making his tour through the southern part of Africa, kept in his possession a dog-faced baboon, to which he gave the name of Kees. He made use of the inquisitive propensity of his ape for the purpose of tasting strange or unknown roots or fruits. Kees would taste all without scruple, and those he rejected were supposed to be either of a disagreeable flavour or a pernicious quality. But whenever the animal met with any favourite root, he was always anxious to secure it for himself, and stemming the ground with his fore-feet, he grasped the plant with his teeth, and pulled out the root by main force. Sometimes, however, his strength applied in that form was not sufficient for the purpose, and then he would have recourse to the expedient of still holding the herbage in his teeth close to the ground, and throwing himself quite over, thus making his body act as a sort of lever, and this mode seldom ever failed to bring up the root.

179. The monkey of the Iacchus genus is a truly remarkable creature, and has some extremely curious habits or instincts. Its manner of capturing all kinds of flies is wonderfully dexterous, and though it seizes upon them so instantaneously, and without any apparent discrimination, it will yet recoil with instinctive and agitating fear from the attempt to clutch a wasp. M. Audouin, of Paris, who had a pair of these animals for sometime in his possession, was satisfied that this fear was the result of an instinctive faculty, and not of experience, as the French species of wasp was quite

different from any these monkeys could have ever seen before. They would, too, dart at the representation of insects in paintings, but would immediately withdraw their paws from that of a wasp, while that of a cat exceedingly alarmed them. These creatures could recognize themselves in a glass as well as others of their own species.

180. Pyrard says that some of the orangs when properly trained and fed will work like servants. They will pound, when ordered, any substance in a mortar: and they are frequently sent to fetch water from the river in small pitchers, which they carry on their heads ; but on arriving at the door of the dwelling, should they suffer the vessel to fall and see it is overturned and broken, they utter their lamentations aloud.

181. Barbot also informs us, that they are frequently rendered of use in some settlements by being taught to turn the spit, and watch the roasting of the meat, which they perform with considerable dexterity and address.

182. M de la Brosse purchased two orangs, which he asserts, would, while in the ship, sit at table and partake of every kind of food. They would use a knife, fork, or spoon, and cut and lay hold of what was on their plates, and drink wine as well as other liquors. At table, when they wanted anything, they easily made themselves understood by the cabin boy, and when he refused to obey their commands, they sometimes became enraged, seized him by the arm, bit, and threw him down. When the male was taken very ill, he required of those around the utmost attention. He was bled twice in the arm, and whenever afterwards he found

himself in the same condition, he held out his arm, as if recollecting that the former operation had proved beneficial.

183. M. Pallavicini, who held an official situation at Batavia, had two orang-otangs in his house, a male and female, which were extremely mild and gentle. They were nearly of the average human height, and they imitated very closely the actions of men, particularly with their hands and arms. In some repects they appeared to be more modest and bashful than savage tribes of people, but this was probably the result of instruction. A female orang was brought alive into Holland from the Island of Borneo, nearly a hundred years ago, and was lodged in the menagerie of the Prince of Orange. At this time she was so young as to be only two feet and a half high. She was very gentle, and exhibited not the slightest symptoms at any time of fierceness or malignity. Her air was melancholy, and her gait grave. She sometimes walked erect. She would eat of almost any kind of food that was given her, but she lived chiefly on bread, roots, and fruit, never showing that voracity so common to most animals of her tribe. She would eat meat that was cooked; she liked eggs, the shells of which she broke with her teeth, and then emptied by sucking out their contents. When strawberries were given to her on a plate, she took them up one by one with a fork, and put them into her mouth, holding at the same time her plate in the other hand. She would take in one hand a vessel containing water, and would drink the contents as calmly as a child or a man. But she did not restrict herself to

water, for she eagerly drank all kinds of wine, particularly Malaga. When she had drunk, she wiped her
lips and used a tooth-pick in the usual manner, if
offered her. Whilst she was on shipboard, she ran freely
about the vessel, and played with the sailors. In the menagerie she frequently played with the blanket which served
her for a bed, and sometimes seemed pleased at tearing
it. She often amused herself also in the room where
she was kept, by climbing on the bars of the window,
as high as the length of her chain would allow. One
day seeing the padlock of her chain opened with
a key and shut again, she seized a little bit of stick and
put it into the key-hole, turning it about in all directions,
trying to see if the padlock could not be opened.
Whether or not she at •length succeeded in her efforts
is matter of doubt, but it is certain that on one occasion
she made her escape from her chain, and was seen to
descend with surprising agility the beams and oblique
rafters of the building. With some trouble she was
re-taken, for she put forth extraordinary muscular power,
and the efforts of four men were found necessary in
order to secure her. Two of them seized her by the
legs, and a third by the head, whilst the other fastened
the collar round her body. During the time she was at
liberty, she had, amongst other pranks, taken a cork
from a bottle of Malaga wine, drunk its contents to the
last drop, and then put the bottle back into its place.
She would present her hand to conduct the people who
came to visit her, and walk as gravely along with them
as if she formed part of the company. She would frequently sit with persons at dinner, when she would

unfold her towel, wipe her lips, use a spoon or a fork in
conveying food to her mouth, **pour liquor into a
glass, and make it touch** that of a person who drank
with her. If invited to take tea, she would bring a cup
and saucer, place them on the table, put in sugar, pour
out the tea, and allow it to cool before she drank it.
All these acts she performed without any other instiga-
tion, than the sign or verbal orders of her master, and
often even of her own accord.

184. An interesting animal of this species was brought
by Captain Methuen, from the south coast of Borneo.
On his arrival in Java from Batavia he was allowed to
be at perfect liberty till within a day or two of being put
on board the Cæsar to be brought to England. While
at large he made no attempt to escape, but became
violent when put into a large railed bamboo cage. As
soon as he felt himself in confinement, he seized the
rails of the cage, shook them violently, and endeavoured
to break them in pieces; but finding, in grasping several,
that they did not yield, he tried them separately, and
having discovered one weaker than the rest, worked at
it energetically and perseveringly till he broke it and
then made his escape. On board ship an attempt was
made to secure him by a chain tied to a strong staple,
when he instantly unfastened it, and ran off with the
chain, dragging it behind, but finding himself troubled
by its length, he coiled it once or twice and threw it over
his shoulders. This feat he often repeated, and when he
found it would not remain on his shoulder he took it in his
mouth. After the failure of several attempts to secure him,
he was allowed to wander freely about the ship, soon be-

came familiar with the sailors, and far surpassed them in agility. They often chased him about the rigging, and gave him opportunities of showing his adroitness in making his escape. On first starting he endeavoured to outstrip his pursuers by mere speed, but when much pressed, would elude them by seizing a loose rope and swinging out of their reach. At other times he would patiently wait on the shrouds, or at the mast-head, till they almost touched him, and then suddenly lower himself to the deck by any rope that was near, or bound along the mainstay from one mast to the other, swinging by his hands, and moving them one over the other. The men often shook the ropes by which he clung with so much violence as to make Captain Methuen fear the orang would fall, but he soon found that the power of the creature's muscles could not be easily overcome. When in playful humour he would often swing within arms length of his pursuer, strike him with his hand, and then bound to a distance. Next to the boatswain, the captain was the orang's most intimate acquaintance. He would always follow him to the mast-head, where the captain often went for the sake of reading undisturbed by the noise of the ship, and having satisfied himself of there being no eatables in his pockets, would lie down by his side, and spreading a top sail over himself, peep from it occasionally to watch the captain's movements. His favourite amusement in Java was in swinging from the branches of trees, in passing from one tree to another, and in climbing over the roofs of houses; on board, by hanging on his arms from the ropes, and in romping with the boys of the ship. He would entice them to play by striking them with his hand as they passed and then bounding from them, but allowing them to overtake him and engage in a mock scuffle, in which he used his hands, feet, and mouth. His first object in attacking any one appeared to be to throw him down, then to secure him with his hands and feet, and then slightly to wound him with his teeth. Of some small monkeys on board from Java, he seems to have taken but little notice. Once he attempted to throw a small cage containing three of them overboard, probably because he had seen food given them of which he could obtain no part. There was, however, reason to suspect that he was less indifferent to their society when free from observation, and the captain was one day summoned to the top-gallant yard of the mizen-mast, to overlook him playing with a young male monkey. Lying on his back, partially covered with the sail, he for some time contemplated with great gravity the gambols of the monkey which bounded over him, but at length he caught him by the tail, and tried to envelope him in his covering. The monkey seemed to dislike the confinement and broke from the orang, but soon renewed its gambols, and although frequently caught, always escaped. The intercourse, however, did not seem to be that of equals, for the orang-otang never con- descended to romp with the monkeys as he did with the boys of the ship; yet they evidently greatly enjoyed his company, for whenever they broke loose they took their way to his resting place, and were often seen lurking about or clandestinely creeping towards him. They did not become gradually more intimate, for they

2 ม

appeared as confidently familiar with him when he was first observed as at the close of their acquaintance. But although so gentle when not exceedingly irritated, the orang-otang could be excited to violent rage, which he expressed by opening his mouth, showing his teeth, and also by seizing and biting those who were within reach. Sometimes, indeed, he seemed almost driven to desperation, and on two or three occasions committed an act which in man would have been called a threatening of suicide. If repeatedly refused an orange, when he attempted to take it, he would shriek violently and swing furiously about the ropes, then return and endeavour to obtain it, but if again refused he would, for some time, roll on the deck like an angry child, uttering the most piercing screams, and then, suddenly starting up, rush furiously over the side of the ship and disappear. When this act was first witnessed it was thought he had thrown himself into the sea, but search being made, he was found concealed under the chains. On two occasions only he exhibited violent alarm, and appeared to seek for safety in gaining as high an elevation as possible. On seeing eight turtles brought on board whilst the Cæsar was off the island of Ascension, he climbed with all possible speed to a higher part of the ship than he had ever before reached, and looking down upon them, shot out his long lips into the form of a hog's snout, and at the same time uttered a sound which might be described as between the grunting of a pig and the croaking of a frog. After some time he ventured to descend, but with great caution, peeping constantly at the turtles, but he could not be induced to approach within many yards of them. He ran to the same height, and uttered the same sounds, on seeing some men bathing and splashing in the sea; and afterwards showed nearly the same degree of fear at the sight of a live tortoise.

185. Of an orang-otang which M. le Compte saw in the straits of Malacea, he says, that all its actions were so imitative of those of mankind, and its passions were so expressive and lively, that a dumb person could scarcely have made himself more clearly understood. This animal was very gentle and affectionate, though it would frequently make a stamping noise with its feet, from anger, as well as joy, when it received, or was refused any kind of food to which it was partial. Its agility was scarcely credible. With the greatest ease and security it would run about amongst the rigging, vaulting from rope to rope, and indulging in a thousand pranks, as if it were delighted at exhibiting its feats for the diversion of the company. Sometimes, suspended by one arm, it would poise itself and then suddenly turn round upon a rope with nearly as much quickness as a wheel on a sling. Sometimes it would slide down one of the ropes and then climb it again with astonishing agility. It seemed as if there were no posture which this animal could not imitate, or any motion that it could not perform. It has even sometimes being known to fling itself downwards from one rope to another. He learned artificial tastes of civilization, and preferred tea and coffee to water; tastes less natural, and more to be regretted, soon followed, for he took to drinking wine, and was so

fond of spirituous liquors, that he was detected in stealing the captain's brandy bottle.

186. One of these animals was for some time the
inmate of a ship, where it became quite companionable,
and gained the affections of the passengers and crew.
So far from exhibiting the sullen and sluggish demeanour which has been attributed to this ape, the siamang
displayed great activity and quickness, skipping about
the ropes, and given to harmless tricks. It took a
fancy to a little Papuan girl who was on board, and
would sit with its arms round her neck, eating biscuits
with her. It was of an inquisitive nature, running up
the rigging, and watching from its elevated position a
passing vessel, and remaining there until the ship was
out of sight. In temper it was rather uncertain, and
apt to fly into a passion if opposed in any wish. When
thus excited, it would fling itself down, just like a
naughty spoiled child, roll about the deck with great
contortion of limbs and face, strike at everything that
came into its way, and scream incessantly with a sound
like Ra! ra! ra.! It had a strange predilection for ink,
and in order to procure this remarkable dainty, would
drain the ink-bottle whenever there was an opportunity
of so doing, or suck the pens in default of the liquid
itself. Being itself destitute of a tail, and fearing no
reprisals in that direction, the siamang used to make
very free with the tails of some monkeys that lived on
board of the same vessel. Catching an unfortunate
monkey by its caudal appendage, away went Ungka, as
the ape was named, dragging the monkey after him along
the deck until the wretched animal writhed itself free

from its tormentor. At another time Ungka would carry the monkey by the tail up the rigging, in spite of its squeaks and struggles, and then quietly let it drop. It was sensitive to ridicule; and when its feelings were hurt, it used to inflate its throat until it resembled a large wen, and looked seriously at the offenders uttering hollow barks at intervals.

187. A few years ago we lived next door to a lady who had a pet monkey which was one of the most imitative and mischievous little beings that ever existed. His imitative nature caused the servants so much trouble that he had not a friend among those of his own house. One day he observed the ladies' maid washing her mistress' lace, and his offers of assistance having been somewhat roughly repulsed by her, chattering and scolding he went forth in search of adventures. Unfortunately my windows were invitingly open, and he entered, with the idea of washing fresh in his head. His spirit of curiosity induced him to open two small drawers from which he abstracted their whole contents, consisting of lace, ribbons, and handkerchiefs. He placed these things in a foot-pan, together with all the water and soap that happened to be in the room, and he must then have washed away with great vigour, for when I returned to my room, after an absence of an hour or so, to my astonishment I found him busily engaged in laundry operations, spreading the torn and disfigured remnants to dry. He was well aware that he was doing wrong, for without any speaking to him, he made off the moment he saw me, going very quickly and hiding himself in the case of the kitchen clock in his own home.

By this act the servants knew he had been doing mischief, as this was his place of refuge when in trouble or
disgrace. One day he watched the cook while she was
preparing some partridges for dinner, and I suppose
that in his own mind he considered that all birds ought
to be so treated, for he managed to get into the yard
where his mistress kept a few pet bantam fowls, and
after robbing them of their eggs, he secured one of the
poor hens with which he proceeded to the kitchen, and
then commenced plucking it. The noise that the poor
bird made, brought some of the servants to the rescue,
but they found it in such a pitiful state that in mercy
it was at once killed. After this outrageous act Mr.
Monkey was chained up, which humiliated him so much,
that he steadily refused his food, and soon died.

188. One of these animals which passed several years
in Europe, was remarkable for its amiable temper ; and
although by no means free from the little mischievous
and pilfering habits that are so inextricably interwoven
in the monkey nature, was so quiet and gentle as to be
left at perfect liberty. He was an adept at unlocking
boxes and examining their contents, could unravel the
intricacies of a knot, and was possessed of a hand dex-
trous and nimble at picking pockets. The last named
occupation seemed to afford peculiar gratification, which
was increased by the fact that his visitors were accustomed to carry nuts, cakes, and other delicacies in their
pockets, on purpose for the monkey to find them there.

# THE HORSE.

——•┼┤•——

Nature, Thy daughter, ever-changing birth
Of Thee the great Immutable, to man
Speaks wisdom ; is his oracle supreme ;
And he who most consults her is most wise.—YOUNG.

189. As may be readily supposed, the intrepidity of
the horse is often of signal service in the cause of
humanity, commanding at once our esteem and admir
ation. We know of no instance in which his assistance
was so successfully rendered as in that which once
occurred at the Cape of Good Hope, and which is related
by M. De Pages in his Travels Round the World. "I
should have found it difficult to give it credit, had it
not happened the evening before my arrival, and if,
besides the public notoriety of the fact, I had not been
an eye-witness of those vehement emotions of sympathy,
blended with admiration, which it had justly excited in
the mind of every individual at the Cape. A violent
gale of wind setting in from north-north-west, a vessel
in the road dragged her anchors, was forced on the
rocks, and bulged, and while a greater part of the crew
fell an immediate sacrifice to the waves, the remainder
were seen from the shore struggling for their lives, by
clinging to the different pieces of the wreck. The sea
ran dreadfully high, and broke over the sailors with

such amazing fury, that no boat whatever could venture off to their assistance. Meanwhile a planter considerably advanced in life, had come from his farm to be a spectator of the shipwreck; his heart was melted at the sight of the unhappy seamen, and knowing the bold and enterprising spirit of his horse, and his particular excellence as a swimmer, he instantly determined to make a desperate effort for their deliverance. He alighted, and blew a little brandy into his horse's nostrils, when again seating himself in the saddle, he instantly pushed into the midst of the breakers. At first both disappeared; but it was not long before they floated on the surface, and swam up to the wreck, when, taking with him two men, each of whom held by one of his boots, he brought them safe to shore. This perilous expedition he repeated no seldomer than seven times, and saved fourteen lives but, on his return the eighth time, his horse being much fatigued, and meeting a most formidable wave, he lost his balance, and was overwhelmed in a moment. The horse swam safely to land; but his gallant rider, alas! was no more."

190. Occasionally, there is so much sagacity and affection combined with the intrepidity of the horse, that his conduct would do credit even to the bravest human nature. He has been known to swim to the assistance of a drowning creature, and this without any other impulse than that of his own generous feelings.—A little girl, the daughter of a gentleman in Warwickshire, playing on the banks of a canal which runs through his grounds, had the misfortune to fall in, and would in all

probability have been drowned, had not a small pony, which had been long kept in the family, plunged into the stream and brought the child safely ashore without the slightest injury.

191 The Surrey iron railway being completed, and opened for the carriage of goods from Wandsworth to Mertsham, a bet was made that a common horse could draw thirty-six tons for six miles along the road, and that he should draw his weight from a dead pull, as well as turn it round the occasional windings of the road. A number of gentlemen assembled near Mertsham to witness this extraordinary triumph of art. Twelve wagons loaded with stones, each wagon weighing about three tons, were chained together, and a horse belonging to Mr. Harwood yoked to the team. He started from near the Fox public-house, and drew the immense chain of wagons, with apparent ease, to near the turnpike at Croydon, a distance of six miles, in one hour and forty-six minutes, which is nearly at the rate of four miles an hour. In the course of the undertaking he was stopped four times, to show that it was not by the impetus of the descent the power was acquired. After each stoppage, a chain of four wagons was added to the cavalcade, with which the same horse again set off with undiminished power. And still farther to show the effect of the railway in facilitating motion, the attending workmen, to the number of about fifty, were directed to mount the wagons; still the horse proceeded without the least distress; and, in truth, there appeared to be scarcely any limitation to the power of his draught. After the trial, the wagons were taken to the

weighing machine, when it was found that the whole weight was little short of fifty-five tons and a half.

192. A gentleman in Buckinghamshire had in his possession, December, 1793, a three years old colt, a dog, and three sheep, which were his constant attendants in all his walks. When the parlour window, which looked into the field, happened to be open, the colt had often been known to leap through it, go up to and caress his master, and then leap back to his pasture.

193. We have ourselves often witnessed similar signs of affection on the part of an old Shetland pony, which would place its forefoot in the hand of its young master like a dog, thrust its head under his arm to be caressed, and join with him and a little terrier in all their noisy rompings on the lawn. The same animal daily bore its master to school and though its heels and teeth were always ready for every aggressive urchin, yet so attached was it to this boy, that it would wait hours for him in his sports by the way, and even walk alone from the stable in town to the school-room, which was fully half a mile distant, and wait saddled and bridled for the afternoon's dismissal.

194. During the Peninsular War, the trumpeter of a French cavalry corps had a fine charger assigned to him, of which he became passionately fond, and which, by gentleness of disposition and uniform docility, equally evinced its affection. The sound of the trumpeter's voice, the sight of his uniform, or the twang of his trumpet, was sufficient to throw this animal into a state of excitement; and he appeared to be pleased and happy only when under the saddle of his rider. Indeed

he was unruly and useless to everybody else; for once on being removed to another part of the forces, and consigned to a young officer, he resolutely refused to perform his evolutions, and bolted to the trumpeter's station, and there took his stand, jostling alongside his former master. This animal, on being restored to the trumpeter, carried him, during several of the Peninsular campaigns, through many difficulties and hair-breadth escapes. At last the corps to which he belonged was worsted, and in the confusion of retreat the trumpeter was mortally wounded. Dropping from his horse, his body was found many days after the engagement stretched on the sward, with the faithful charger standing beside it. During the long interval, it seems that he had never quitted the trumpeter's side, but had stood sentinel over his corps, scaring away the birds of prey, and remaining totally heedless of his own privations. When found, he was in a sadly reduced condition, partly from loss of blood through wounds, but chiefly from want of food, of which in the excess of his grief, he could no be prevailed on to partake.

195. On the evening of Saturday, the 24th February, 1830, Mr Smith, supervisor of excise at Beauly, was proceeding home from a survey of Fort Augustus, and, to save a distance of about sixteen miles, he took the hill road from Drumnadrochit to Beauly. The road was completely blocked up with and indiscernible amidst the waste of snow, so that Mr. Smith soon lost all idea of his route. In this dilemma he thought it best to trust to his horse, and loosening the reins, allowed him to choose his own course. The animal made way,

though slowly and cautiously, till coming to a ravine
near Glenconvent, when both horse and rider suddenly
disappeared in a snow wreath several fathoms deep.
Mr. Smith, on recovering, found himself nearly three
yards from the dangerous spot, with his faithful horse
standing over him, and licking the snow from his face.
He thinks the bridle must have been attached to his
person  So completely, however, had he lost all sense
of consciousness, that beyond the bare fact as stated,
he had no knowledge of the means by which he had
made so striking and providential an escape.

196. Very similar to the above is the following
instance related of a hunter belonging to a farmer in
the neighbourhood of Edinburgh :— On one occasion
his master was returning home from a jovial meeting,
where he had been very liberal in his potations, which
destroyed his power of preserving his equilibrium, and
rendered him at the same time somewhat drowsy. He
had the misfortune to fall from his saddle, but in so
easy a manner, that it had not the effect of rousing him
from his sleepy fit; and he felt quite contented to rest
where he had alighted. His faithful steed, on being
eased of his burden, instead of scampering home, as
one would have expected from his habits, (which were
somewhat vicious,) stood by his prostrate master, and
kept a strict watch over him. The farmer was discovered by some labourers at sunrise, very contentedly
snoozing on a heap of stones by the road side. They
naturally approached to replace him on his saddle; but
every attempt to come near him was resolute opposed

by the grinning teeth and ready heels of his faithful and determined guardian.

197. A farmer who lives in the neighbourhood of Belford, and regularly attends the markets there, was returning home one evening in 1828, and being somewhat tipsy, rolled off his saddle into the middle of the road. His horse stood still; but after remaining patiently for some time, and not observing any disposition in its rider to get up and proceed further, he took him by the collar and shook him. This had little or no effect, for the farmer only gave a grumble of dissatisfaction at having his repose disturbed. The animal was not to be put off with any such evasion, and so applied his mouth to one of his master's coat laps, and after several attempts by dragging at it, to raise him upon his feet, the coat lap gave way. Three individuals who witnessed this extraordinary proceeding then went up, and assisted him in mounting his horse, putting the one coat lap into the pocket of the other, when he trotted off, and safely reached home. This horse is deservedly a favourite of his master, and has, we understand, occasionally been engaged in gambols with him like a dog.

198. A person near Boston, in America, was in the habit, whenever he wished to catch his horse in the field, of taking a quantity of corn in a measure by way of bait. On calling to him, the horse would come up and eat the corn, while the bridle was put over his head. But the owner having deceived the animal several times, by calling him when he had no corn in the measure, the horse at length began to suspect the

N

design; and coming up one day as·usual, on being called, looked into the measure, and seeing it empty, turned round, reared on his hind-legs, and killed his master on the spot.

199. A baronet, one of whose hunters had never tired in the longest chase, once encouraged the cruel thought of attempting completely to fatigue him. After a long chase, therefore, he dined, and again mounting, rode furiously among the hills. When brought to the stable his strength appeared exhausted, and he was scarcely able to walk. The groom, possessed of more feeling than his brutal master, could not refrain from tears at the sight of so noble an animal thus sunk down. The baronet some time after entered the stable, when the horse made a furious spring upon him, and had not the groom interfered, would soon have put it out of his power of ever again misusing his animals.

200. It is told of a horse belonging to an Irish noble-man, that he had become restive and furious whenever a certain individual came into his presence. One day this poor fellow happened to pass within reach, when the animal seized him with its teeth and broke his arm; it then threw him down, and lay upon him—every effort to get it off proving unavailing, till the bystanders were compelled to shoot it. The reason assigned for this ferocity was, that the man had performed a cruel operation on the animal some time before, and which it seems to have revengefully remembered.

201. My neighbour's horse, says White of Selborne, will not only not stay by himself abroad, but he will not bear to be left alone in a strange stable without dis-

covering the utmost impatience, and endeavouring to break the rack and manger with his forefeet. He has been known to leap out at a stable-window after company; and yet in other respects he is remarkable quiet.

202. A gentleman of Bristol had a greyhound, which slept in the stable along with a very fine hunter of about five years of age. These animals became mutually attached, and regarded each other with the most tender affection. The greyhound always lay under the manger beside the horse, which was so fond of him, that he became unhappy and restless when the dog was out of his sight. It was a common practice with the gentleman to whom they belonged to call at the stable for the greyhound to accompany him in his walk: on such occasions the horse would look over his shoulder at the dog with much anxiety, and neigh in a manner which plainly said—" Let me also accompany you." When the dog returned to the stable, he was always welcomed by a loud neigh—he ran up to the horse and licked his nose ; in return, the horse would scratch the dog's back with his teeth. One day, when the groom was out with the horse and greyhound for exercise, a large dog attacked the latter, and quickly bore him to the ground ; on which the horse threw back his ears, and, in spite of all efforts of the groom, rushed at the strange dog that was worrying at the greyhound, seized him by the back with his teeth, which speedily made him quit his hold, and shook him till a large piece of skin gave way. The offender no sooner got on his feet, than he judged it prudent to beat a precipitate retreat from so formidable an opponent

203. The island of Krütsand, which is formed by two
branches of the Elbe, is frequently under water, when,
at the time of the spring-tides, the wind has blown in a
direction contrary to that of the current. In April,
1796, the water one day rose so rapidly, that the horses
which were grazing in the plain, with their foals, suddenly found themselves standing in deep water, upon
which they all set up a loud neighing, and collected
themselves together within a small extent of ground.
In this assembly they seemed to determine upon the
following prudent measure, as the only means of saving
their young foals, that were now standing up to the
belly in the flood ; in the execution of which some old
mares also took a principal part, which could not be
supposed to have been influenced by any maternal
solicitude for the safety of the young. The method
they adopted was this : every two horses took a foal
between them, and pressing their sides together, kept
it wedged in, and lifted up quite above the surface of
the water. All the horned cattle in the vicinity had
already set themselves afloat, and were swimming in
regular columns towards their homes. But these noble
steeds, with undaunted perseverance, remained immovable under their cherished burdens for the space
of six hours, till the tide ebbing, the water subsided,
and the foals were at length placed out of danger. The
inhabitants, who had rowed to the place in boats, viewed
with delight this singular manœuvre, whereby their
valuable foals were·preserved from a destruction otherwise inevitable.

204. Even great disparity of kind does not always prevent social advances and mutual fellowship; for a very intelligent and observant person has assured me, that in the former part of his life, keeping but one horse, he happened also on a time to have one solitary hen. These two incongruous animals spent much of their time together in a lonely orchard, where they saw no creatures but each other. By degrees an apparent regard began to take place between these two sequestered individuals. The fowl would approach the quadruped with notes of complacency, rubbing herself quietly against his legs, whilst the horse would look down with satisfaction, and move with the greatest caution and circumspection, lest he should trample on his diminutive companion. Thus, by mutual good offices, each seemed to console the vacant hours of the other; so that Milton, when he puts the following sentiment in the mouth of Adam, seems somewhat mistaken—

"Much less can bird with beast, or fish with fowl
So well converse, nor with the ox the ape."

205. Dr. Smith, of the Queen's County Militia, Ireland, had a beautiful hackney, which, although extremely spirited, was at the same time wonderfully docile. He had also a fine Newfoundland dog, named Cæsar. These animals were mutually attached, and seemed perfectly acquainted with each other's actions. The dog was always kept in the stable at night, and universally lay beside the horse. When Dr. Smith practised in Dublin, he visited his patients on horseback, and had no other servant to take care of the horse, while in their houses, but Cæsar, to whom he gave the reins in his mouth.

2 N

The horse stood very quietly, even in that crowded city, beside his friend Cæsar. When it happened that the doctor had a patient not far distant from the place where he paid his last visit, he did not think it worth while to remount, but called to his horse and Cæsar. They both instantly obeyed, and remained quietly opposite the door where he entered, until he came out again. While he remained in Maryborough, Queen's County, where I commanded a detachment, I had many opportunities of witnessing the friendship and sagacity of these intelligent animals. The horse seemed to be as implicitly obedient to his friend Cæsar as he could possibly be to his groom. The doctor would go to the stable, accompanied by his dog, put the bridle upon his horse, and giving the reins' to Cæsar, bid him take the horse to the water. They both understood what was to be done, when off trotted Cæsar, followed by the horse, which frisked, capered, and played with the dog all the way to the rivulet, about three hundred yards distant from the stable. We followed at a great distance, always keeping as far off as possible, so that we could observe their manœuvres. They invariably went to the stream, and after the horse had quenched his thirst, both returned in the same playful manner as they had gone out. The doctor frequently desired Cæsar to make the horse leap over this stream, which might be about six feet broad. The dog, by a kind of bark, and leaping up towards the horse's head, intimated to him what he wanted, which was quickly understood, and he cantered off, preceded by Cæsar, and took the leap in a neat and regular style. The dog was then desired a great deal of spirit. One day, as he was passing near a town of considerable size which lay on the line of road, the volunteers were at drill on the common ; and the instant that Solus, (for that was the name of the horse) heard the drum, he leaped the fence, and was speedily at that post in front of the volunteers which would have been occupied by the commanding officer of a regiment on parade or at drill ; nor could the rider by any means get him off the ground until the volunteers retired to the town. As long as they kept the field, the horse took the proper place of a command-ing officer in all their manœuvres, and he marched at the head of the corps into the town, prancing in military style as cleverly as his stiffened legs would allow him, to the great amusement of the volunteers and spectators, and to the no small annoyance of the clerk, who did not feel very highly honoured by Solus making a colonel of him against his will.

214. A cart-horse belonging to Mr. Leggat, Gallow-gate-Street, Glasgow, had been several times cured by Mr. Downie, farrier there. He had not, however, been troubled with disease for a considerable time, but on a recurrence of the disorder, he happened one morning to be employed in College-Street, a distance of nearly a mile from Mr. Downie's workshop. Arranged in a row with other horses engaged in the same work, while the carters were absent, he left the range, and unattended by any driver, went down the High-Street, along the Gallowgate, and up a narrow lane, where he stopped at the farrier's door. As neither Mr. Leggat nor any one appeared with the horse, it was surmised that he had

been seized with his old complaint. Being unyoked
from the cart, he lay down and showed by every means
of which he was capable that he was in distress. He
was again treated as usual, and sent home to his master,
who had by that time persons in all directions in search
of him.

215. Mr. Astley, junior, of the Royal Amphitheatre,
Westminster Bridge, once had in his possession a remarkably fine Barbary horse, forty-three years of age,
which was presented him by the Duke of Leeds. This
celebrated animal for a number of years officiated in
the character of a waiter in the course of the performances at the amphitheatre, and at various other
theatres in the United Kingdom. At the request of his
master, he would ungirth his own saddle, wash his feet
in a pail of water, and would also bring into the riding-
school a tea-table and its appendages, which feat was
usually followed up by fetching a chair, or stool, or whatever might be wanted. His achievements were generally
wound up by his taking a kettle of boiling water from a
blazing fire, to the wonder and admiration of the spectators. Ray affirms that he has seen a horse that danced
to music, which at the command of his master affected
to be lame, feigned death, lay motionless with his limbs
extended, and allowed himself to be dragged about till
some words were pronounced, when he instantly sprang
to his feet. Feats of this kind are now indeed common,
and must have been witnessed by many of our readers
in the circuses of Astley, Ord, Ducrow, and others.
Dancing, embracing, lying down to make sport with
their keepers, fetching cane and gloves, selecting pecu-

liar cards, and many similar performances, are among
the expected entertainments of all equestrian exhibitions.

216. A few years ago, one of the most attractive of
Ducrow's exhibitions was " The Muleteer and his Wonderful Horse." The feats of this pair are pleasantly
described in a popular journal, by an individual who
witnessed them in 1838 :—" The horse," says this writer,
" is a beautiful piebald, perfect almost in mould, and
adorned about the neck with little bells. At first, it
playfully and trickishly avoids its master when he affects
an anxiety to catch it; but when the muleteer averts
his head, and assumes the appearance of sullenness,
the animal at once stops, and comes up close to his
side, as if very penitent for its untimely sportiveness.
Its master is pacified, and after caressing it a little, he
touches the animal's fore-legs. It stretches them out,
and, in doing so, necessarily causes the hind legs to
project also. We now see the purpose of these movements. The muleteer wishes a seat, and an excellent
one he finds upon the horse's protruded *hind-legs*. A
variety of instances of docility similar to this, are exhibited by the creature in succession, but its leaping feats
appeared to us the most striking of all. Poles are
brought into the ring, and the horse clears *six* of these,
one after the other, with a distance of not more than
four feet between! After it has done this, it goes up
*limping* to its master, as if to say, 'See, I can do no
more to night!' The muleteer lifts the lame foot, and
seems to search for the cause of the halt, but in vain.
Still, however, the horse goes on limping. The mule-

teer then looks it in the face, and shakes his head, as if he would say, 'Ah! you are shamming, you rogue; arn't you?' And a sham it proves to be; for, at a touch of the whip, the creature bounds off like a fawn, sound both in wind and limb."

217. One of the earliest equine actors in this country was Banks's celebrated horse " Morocco," alluded to by Shakespeare in Love's Labour Lost, and by other writers of that time. It is stated of this animal that he would restore a glove to its owner after his master had whispered the man's name in his ear, and that he would tell the number of pence in any silver coin. He danced likewise to the sound of a pipe, and told money with his feet.

218. M. le Gendre mentions similar feats performed by a small horse at the fair of St. Germains in 1732. Among others which he accomplished with astonishing precision, he could specify, by striking his foot so many times on the ground, the number of marks upon a card which any person present had drawn out of a pack. He could also tell the hour and minute to which the hands of a watch pointed in a similar manner. His master collected a number of coins from different persons in the company, mixed them together, and threw them to the horse in a handkerchief. The animal took it in his mouth, and delivered to each person his own piece of money. What is still more wonderful, considering his size, weight, and peculiarity of construction, the horse had been known to pass along the tight-rope.

219. It is recorded that at the solemnities which attended the wedding of Robert, brother to the king of

France,,in 1237, a horse was ridden along a rope, and that it kept its balance and moved with precision. Our surprise at this rope-dancing faculty may, however, be a little abated, when we learn that the more unwieldy elephant has actually exhibited the same performance.

220. In 1794, a gentleman had a horse which, after being kept up in the stable for some time, and turned out into a field where there was a pump well supplied with water, regularly obtained a quantity therefrom by his own dexterity. For this purpose the animal was observed to take the handle into his mouth, and work it with the head, in a way exactly similar to that done by the hand of man, until a sufficiency was procured.

221. Again, horses have been taught to go to and from water or pasture by themselves, open the gate, and otherwise to conduct themselves with a propriety almost human.

222. We have ourselves known a farm boy, who was too small to mount the plough horses, teach one of the team to put down its head to the ground, allow him to get astride its neck, and then, by gently elevating the head, to let him slip backwards to his seat on its back. This act we have seen done by the same horse a hundred times, and there was no doubt that the animal perfectly understood the wishes of the boy, and the use of its lowering the head for the purpose of his mounting.

223. M. de Boussanelle, a captain of cavalry in the regiment of Beauvilliers, mentions that a horse belonging to his company being, from age, unable to eat his hay or grind his oats, was fed for two months by two horses on his right and left, who ate with him. These

two chargers, drawing the hay out of the racks, chewed
it, and put it before the old horse, and did the same
with the oats, which he was then able to eat.

224. In 1828, Mr. Evans of Henfaes, Montgomery-
shire, had a favourite pony mare and colt, that grazed
in a field adjoining the Severn. One day the pony
made her appearance in front of the house, and, by
clattering with her feet and other noises, attracted
attention. Observing this, a person went out, and she
immediately galloped off. Mr. Evans desired that she
should be followed; and all the gates from the house
to the field were found to have been forced open. On
reaching the field, the pony was found looking into the
river, over the spot where the colt was lying drowned.

225. Forrester, the famous racer, had triumphed in
many a severe contest; at length, overweighted and
overmatched, the rally had commenced. His adversary,
who had been waiting behind, was quickly gaining upon
him; he reared, and eventually got abreast: they
continued so till within the distance. They were
parallel; but the strength of Forrester began to fail.
He made a last desperate plunge, seized his opponent
by the jaw to hold him back, and it was with great
difficulty he could be forced to quit his hold. Forrester,
however, lost the race.

226. In 1753, Mr. Quin had a racer which entered into
the spirit of the course as much as his master. One
day, finding his rival gradually passing him, he seized
him by the legs, and both riders were obliged to dis-
mount, in order to separate the infuriated animals, now
engaged with each other in most deadly conflict.

227. A friend of mine was one dark night riding home through a wood, and had the misfortune to strike his head against the branch of a tree, and fell from his horse stunned by the blow. The horse immediately returned to the house which they had left, about a mile distant. He found the door closed, and the family gone to bed. He pawed at the door, till one of them, hearing the noise, arose and opened it, and to his surprise saw the horse of his friend. No sooner was the door opened than the horse turned round, and the man suspecting there was something wrong, followed the animal, which led him directly to the spot where his master lay on the ground in a faint.

228. Equal in point of sagacity with this was the conduct of an old horse belonging to a carter in Strath-miglo, Fifeshire. The carter having a large family, this animal had got particularly intimate with the children, and would on no account move when they were playing among his feet, as if it feared to do them injury. On one occasion, when dragging a loaded cart through a narrow lane near the village, a young child happened to be playing in the road, and would inevitably have been crushed by the wheels, had it not been for the sagacity of this animal. He carefully took it by the clothes with his teeth, carried it for a few yards, and then placed it on a bank by the wayside, moving slowly all the while, and looking back, as if to satisfy himself that the wheels of the cart had cleared it. This animal was one of the most intelligent of his kind, and performed his duties with a steadiness and precision that were perfectly surprising.

o

229. Mr. Pringle, farmer, of Nisbit Hill, rides upon a horse to Dunse railway station, a distance of about two miles, and when he dismounts, he orders his horse to go home, whereupon it turns and walks off at a slow pace. Notwithstanding the cross roads, it finds its way home.

230. The writer knows a pony that is in the habit of running in the lanes, that can and does open the field gates where it finds a better pasturage than in the lanes.

231. A friend of the writer's was appointed to the situation of district traveller for a Manchester house; the person he succeeded had been in the habit of taking his glass pretty freely, (for which he was discharged), and his horse for the first three or four rounds, much to the annoyance of my friend, stopped at every house his master had been in the habit of stopping at.

232. With proper treatment and due care, Shetland ponies become the most docile and fine-tempered animals in the world, but if once they are badly used they soon become as full of tricks and as vicious as a monkey. The only bad habit of which I could never break ours, was opening every gate which hindered his getting out. There was scarcely any common fastening which he could not undo with his teeth, and if he found a weak place in railings, he would push against it till he broke it, and then gallop away for an hour or two where he chose. He also had a peculiar knack of finding out and opening the oak-chest in any stable. When on a marauding excursion of this kind, he knew perfectly well he was doing wrong, and would not let me catch him, although

at home he would follow me anywhere, putting his nose into my hand to ask for apples or bread. At all times, however, he allowed any one of the children, particularly my little girl, to catch him, and when caught always came back as quietly as possible. There was a great deal of fun and conscious roguery in the little fellow's style of mischief, which I could never help laughing at. When idle in his field, nothing seemed to please him so much as a game of romps with any dog who would play with him. When I lived close to Nairn, as soon as ever he heard the horn of the mail-coach, which was blown on its arrival at the inn, he invariably ran to an elevated part in the field, from which he could see over the wall, and waited there for the mail to pass. As soon as it came opposite his station off he set, galloping round and round the field, with his heels generally higher than his head, and his long mane and tail streaming out, evidently showing himself off to obtain the applause of the passengers, to whom he seemed to afford daily amusement, as every head was turned back to see him as long as they possibly could.

233. There is an interesting fact related of the hero of Poland, indicative of his customary practice of alms-giving. Wishing to convey a present to a clerical friend, he gave the commission to a young man of the name of Jelmer, desiring him to take the horse he usually rode. On his return, the messenger informed Kosciusko that he would never again ride his horse, unless he gave him his purse at the same time; and on the latter enquiring what he meant, he replied: "As soon as a poor man on the road takes of his hat and asks charity, the

animal immediately stands still, and will not stir till
something is bestowed upon the petitioner; and as I
had no money about me, I had to feign giving in order
to satisfy the horse, and induce him to proceed."

234. Every one knows the esprit de corps the horse
displays in following the hounds, but whether this arises
from an innate love of the chace, or from the communication to him of the spirit that he perceives to be actu-
ating his rider and others about him, we cannot tell ;
something of the same feeling actuates him in other
acquired habits, and Colonel Smith has related the
following affecting instance of attachment either to the
men who had been his companions, or the habits he
had acquired, in a charger which had been the property
of General Sir Robert Gillespie. When he fell at the
storming of Kalunga, his favourite black charger, bred
at the Cape of Good Hope, and carried by him to India,
was, at the sale of his effects, competed for by several
officers of his division, and finally knocked down to the
privates of the 8th dragoons, who contributed their
prize money, to the amount of £500. sterling, to retain
this commemoration of their late commander. Thus
the charger was always led at the head of the regiment
on a march, and at the station of Cawnpore was usually
indulged with taking his ancient post at the colour
stand, where the salute of passing squadrons was given
at drill and on reviews. When the regiment was ordered
home, the funds of the privates remaining low, he was
bought for the same sum by a relative of ours, who pro
vided funds and a paddock for him, where he might
end his days in comfort; but when the corps·had

marched, and the sound of the trumpet had departed,
he refused to eat; and on the first opportunity, being
led out to exercise, he broke from his groom, and
galloping to his ancient station on the parade, after
neighing aloud, dropped down and died.

235. A horse in the depôt at Woolwich had proved so
unmanageable to the rough-riders, that, at length, no
one among them durst even venture to mount him. His
mode of throwing or dismounting his rider consisted in
lying down and rolling over him, or else crushing his
leg against some wall, or post, or paling. All means to
break him of these perilous tricks proving unavailing,
the animal was brought before the commanding officer,
with the character of being " incurably vicious," and
with a recommendation, on that account, that he should
be " cast," and sold out of his majesty's service. Colonel
Quest, hearing of this, and knowing the horse to be
thorough-bred, and one of the best actioned and cleverest
horses in the regiment, besought the commanding officer
to permit him to be transferred into the riding troop.
This was consented to, and the transfer was no sooner
accomplished, than Colonel Quest determined to pursue
a system of management directly opposite to that which
had been already attempted. He had him led daily
into the riding-school—suffered no whip ever to be
shown to him while there, but patted him and tried to
make him execute this and the other manœuvre; and as
afterwards he proved obedient, rewarded him with a
handful of corn or beans, or a piece of bread, with which
bribes his pockets were invariably well supplied. In
this manner, and in no great distance of time, was the

rebel not only subdued and tamed, but rendered so
perfectly quiet that a little child could ride him. He
became at length taught to kneel down while his rider
mounted, and to perform various evolutions, dances, and
tricks in the manger, which no other horse in the school
could be brought to do. In fine, so great a favourite
did be become, that his master gave him the appellation
of " The Darling."

236. A gentleman who was in possession of an exceedingly vicious hunter, happened to be relating some
of his bad propensities, to a party of friends at dinner,
and among these he mentioned the difficulty there was
in trimming his heels. It was never to be accomplished
without the aid of several assistants, and even then was
attended with great difficulty and danger. During this
conversation, in which he defied any of his friends to
perform the task, he had forgotten that his youngest
child, a boy of about three years of age, was present.
This juvenile Nimrod had been by no means the in-
attentive observer which might have been expected
from his tender years, for on the next morning in
passing through the stable, the father descried to his
unspeakable horror, his infant busily employed with a
pair of scissors clipping the heels of this outrageous
brute. The horse instead of exhibiting his usual
determined resistance to the operation, was looking
round with the greatest complacency on his pigmy
groom, whom the parent expected to see struck dead at
his feet. At his father's call, however, he crept away
from the animal altogether unharmed. No money
would have bought this noble creature from the

delighted father. Soon afterwards, when returning from a party in which he had been too liberal in his potations, he slipped from his saddle, and falling tolerably easily, went comfortably to sleep on the road side. This faithful fellow, instead of scampering home, stood by his prostrate master; and by threatening with his teeth and with his heels, kept every one from him until he had regained sufficient sense once more to seat himself in the saddle, and proceed home.

237. The tameness of animals on Sundays, in countries where the day is strictly observed, as contrasted with their comparative wildness on other days, is, I think, so remarkable as scarcely to admit of a doubt. As it can scarcely be imagined that their instinct can lead them to mark the regular recurrence of the day, and their immunity during it from pursuit and danger, it must probably be accounted for by the fact that, labour being suspended, a general stillness pervades the country, insensibly conveying to their minds a sense of security. Domestic animals, however, and those particularly which are most closely associated with us, and as it were form part of our families, become, I am persuaded, perfectly aware of the regular advent of Sunday, and not unfrequently shew that this is the case, by voluntarily adapting themselves to the requirements of the day. There would probably be no difficulty in collecting a sufficiency of instances in support of this theory to establish it, but I will just mention the following which happens to occur to me. The carriage-horses of a friend of mine, were accustomed on week-days to take their mistress out for an early drive before

luncheon, while on the Sundays they enjoyed a perfect rest. On the week-days, they never thought of lying down in the morning before the time they usually went out, but on Sunday mornings they invariably did so, as if determined to make the most of their day's rest. I supposed that they might have been induced to do this in consequence of their beds being made up earlier on those days, or of some other departure from the usual routine of the stable arrangements, but I was told that no variation of the kind was ever made.

238. The following is an instance of retentiveness of memory in a horse. I was the happy owner of a grey pony, when stationed at Ferozepore, in 1841. In November of that year I left that station, accompanied by my gallant grey, and was absent in Afghanistan fourteen months. On my return, I galloped into the station by the road in which I knew my bungalow was situated, and looked about, trying to recognise the place, but owing to additions to the house, and alterations in the garden and neighbouring houses and grounds, I failed in the effort. Not so my pony, who, whilst I was staring about at the many new houses which had been built, and at the increase of the place in one year, very nearly unshipped me by turning sharply into the accustomed gateway which stood invitingly open.

239. Their friendships are sometimes incongruous; and so are the friendships of man. The opposites in temper and pursuits occasionally associate with and love each other; and the very opposition of character now and then constitutes the bond of friendship. O'Kelly's Duncannon formed an intense friendship

with a sheep. He would lift it into the manger to share his fodder, and would suffer no one to offer it the least molestation. Chillaby, the mad Arabian, whom only one groom dared to approach, had also his peculiar attachment for a lamb ; and the little protégé used to employ itself during many an hour in batting away the flies from his nobler friend. The Darley Arabian imbibed a friendship for a cat, which sat upon his back, or nestled as closely to him as she could ; and when he died, she pined away and died too. A farmer's boy had fed and taken great care of a colt. He was working one day in the field, when he was furiously pursued by a vicious bull. The boy ran to a ditch, and got into it just as the bull was close upon him. The furious beast endeavoured to gore him, and would probably have succeeded, had not the colt come to his assistance. This little animal attacked the bull, screaming with rage as he did it, when some labourers who were working near the place, hearing the strange outcry, ran to see what was the matter, and extricated the boy from danger.

240. During the past week a horse belonging to Mr. Jeffcoat, farmer, of Bishop's Itchington, was taken with another to work upon the farm. The ground was very slippery, and on becoming disengaged from the team, it immediately made for the village blacksmith's shop, no doubt with a view of being " roughed," and this operation having been performed, the animal returned home unattended.

241. Among the incidents current, is a singular instance of sagacity evinced by a pony in the pit at the

2 o

time of the explosion. This little animal, which stands
only three feet and a few inches in height, was employed
by the stonemasons, and was driven by a boy of the
name of Proud. After the shock of the explosion, the
boy was found clinging to its neck, and on his being
taken away by the escaping party, the pony followed
them, but on a new difficulty presenting itself which
necessitated the men and boys to crawl, it was thought
that the pony must be left behind. From the almost
human whining of the diminutive creature, however, the
boy was induced to put his handkerchief around his
neck, and assist to drag it forward. On his getting into
the cage his little charge followed him also, and was
with him drawn safely to the bank.

242. M. Arnauld, in his History of Animals, relates
the following incident of ferocious courage in a mule.
This animal belonged to a gentleman in Florence, and
became so vicious and refractory, that he not only refused to submit to any kind of labour, but actually
attacked with his heels and teeth those who attempted
to compel him. Wearied with such conduct, his master
resolved to make away with him, by exposing him to
the wild beasts in the menagerie of the grand duke.
For this purpose he was first placed in the dens of the
hyenas and tigers, all of whom he would have soon destroyed, had he not been speedly removed. At last he
was handed over to the lion, but the mule, instead of
exhibiting any symptoms of alarm, quietly receded to a
corner, keeping his front opposed to his adversary.
Once planted in the corner, he resolutely kept his place,
eyeing every movement of the lion, which was preparing

to spring upon him. The lion, however, perceiving the difficulty of an attack, practised all his wiles to throw the mule off his guard, but in vain. At length the latter peceiving an opportunity, made a sudden rush upon the lion, and in an instant broke several of his teeth by the stroke of his fore-feet. The "king of the animals," as he had been called, finding that he had got quite enough of the combat, slunk grumbling to his cage, and left the hardy mule master of the battle.

# THE ASS.

———•{}•———

To him who in the love of nature holds
Communion with her visible forms, she speaks
A various language; for his gayer hours
She has a voice of gladness, and a smile
And eloquence of beauty, and she glides
Into his darker musings, with a mild
And healing sympathy, that steals away
Their sharpness, ere he is aware.—Bryant.

243. An old man, who a few years ago sold vegetables
in London, used in his employment an ass, which conveyed his baskets from door to door. Frequently he
gave the poor industrious creature a handful of hay, or
a piece of bread, or greens, by way of refreshment and
reward. He had no need of any goad for the animal,
and seldom indeed had he to lift up his hand to drive it
on. His kind treatment was one day remarked to him,
and he was asked whether his beast were apt to be stub-
born. "Ah! master," replied he, "it is of no use to be
cruel, and as for stubbornness, I cannot complain; for
he is ready to do anything, and go anywhere. I bred
him myself. He is sometimes skittish and playful, and
once ran away from me; you will hardly believe it, but
there were more than fifty people after him, yet he
turned back of himself, and never stopped till he ran
his head kindly into my bosom."

244. At Salwall, in 1825, an ass was ferociously attacked by a bull-dog; but the poor animal defended himself so gallantly with his heels—keeping his rear always presented to his assailant—that the dog was unable to fix on him. He at length turned rapidly round on his adversary, and caught hold of him with his teeth in such a manner that the dog was unable to retaliate. Here the dog howled most repentantly, and one would have thought that the ass would have dismissed him with this punishment; but no: he dragged the enemy to the river Derwent, into which he put him over the head, and lying down upon him, kept him under water till he was drowned.

215. In 1816, an ass belonging to Captain Dundas, then at Malta, was shipped on board the Ister frigate, bound from Gibraltar to that island. The vessel struck on a sand-bank off Cape de Gat, and the ass was thrown overboard, in the hope that it might be able to swim to land, of which, however, there seemed little chance, for the sea was running so high, that a boat which left the ship was lost. A few days after, when the gates of Gibraltar were opened in the morning, the guard was surprised by the ass presenting himself for admittance. On entering, he proceeded immediately to the stable of his former master. The poor animal had not only swam safely to shore, but, without guide, compass, or travelling map, had found his way from Cape de Gat to Gibraltar, a distance of more than two hundred miles—through a mountainous and intricate country, intersected by streams, which he had never traversed before, and in so short a time that he could not have made one false turn.

# THE CAT.

——•♦ ‡ ✖ ‡ •♦——

<blockquote>
Go, from the creatures thy instructions take ;<br>
Learn from the birds what food the thickets yield;<br>
Learn from the beasts, the physic of the field :<br>
The arts of building from the bee receive;<br>
Learn of the mole to plow, the worm to weave;<br>
Learn of the little Nautilus to sail,<br>
Spread the thin oar, and catch the driving gale.—Pope.
</blockquote>

246. A gentleman in the neigbourhood of London had a tortoise-shell cat, which, though he never fed it, or paid much attention to it, formed an attachment for him equal to that of a dog. It knew his ring at the bell, and at whatever time he came home, it was rubbing against his legs long before the servant came, saw him into the sitting room, and then walked off. It was a very active animal, and usually went bird-catching during the night; and when its master rose, which was generally early in the morning, the cat was always ready to receive him at the door of his room, and accompanied him in his morning walk in the garden, alternately skipping to the tops of the trees, and descending and gambolling about him. When he was in his study, it used to pay him several visits in the day, always short ones; but it never retired till he had recognised it. If rubbing against his legs had not the desired

effect, it would mount the writing-table, nudge his shoulder, and if that would not do, pat him on the cheek; but the moment he had shaken it by the paw, and given it a pat or two on the head, it walked off. When he was indisposed, it paid him several visits every day, but never continued in the room; and although it was fond of society generally, and also of its food, it never obtruded its company during meals. Its attachment was thus quite disinterested, and no pains whatever had been taken to train it.

247. When M Sonnini was in Egypt, he had an Angora cat, which remained in his possession for a long time. This animal was one of the most beautiful of its kind, and equally attractive in its manners and dispositions. In Sonnini's solitary moments, she chiefly kept by his side; she interrupted him frequently in the midst of his labours or meditations, by little affecting caresses, and generally followed him in his walks. During his absence, she sought and called for him incessantly, with the utmost inquietude; and if it were long before he re-appeared, she would quit his apartment, and attach herself to the person of the house where he lived, for whom, next to himself, she entertained the greatest affection. She recognised his voice at a distance, and seemed on each fresh meeting with him to feel increased satisfaction. Her gait was frank, and her look as gentle as her character. She possessed, in a word, the disposition of the most amiable dog beneath the brilliant fur of a cat. "This animal," says M. Sonnini, "was my principal amusement for several years. How was the expression of her attachment depicted upon her coun-

tenance! How many times have her tender caresses
made me forget my troubles, and consoled me in my
misfortunes! My beautiful and interesting companion
at length perished. After several days of suffering,
during which I never forsook her, her eyes, constantly
fixed on me, were at length extinguished; and her loss
rent my heart with sorrow."

248. I remember, says a female correspondent, there
was a cat with her kittens found in a hole in the
wall, in the garden of the house where my father-in-law
lived. One of the kittens, being a very beautiful black
one, was brought into the house, and almost immediately attached himself in a very extraordinary way to
me. I was in mourning at the time, and perhaps the
similarity of the hue of my dress to his sable fur might
first have attracted him; but however this may have
been, whenever he came into the room he constantly
jumped into my lap, and evinced his fondness by purring and rubbing his head against me in a very coaxing
manner. He continued thus to distinguish me during
the rest of his life, and though I went with my father-
in-law's family every winter to Dublin, and every summer to the country, the change of abode (to which cats
are supposed so averse) never troubled my favourite,
provided he could be with me. Frequently, when we
have been walking home after spending the evening
out, he has come running down half the street to meet
us, testifying the greatest delight. On one occasion,
when I had an illness which confined me for upwards of
two months to my room, poor Lee Boo deserted the
parlour altogether, though he had been always patted

and caressed by every one there. He would sit for
hours mewing disconsolately at my door, and when he
could, he would steal in, jump upon the bed, testifying
his joy at seeing me by loud purring and coaxing, and
sometimes licked my hand. The very day I went down,
he resumed his regular attendance in the parlour.

249. Madame Helvetius had a favourite cat, which constantly lay at her feet, seemingly always ready to defend
her. It never molested the birds which its mistress
kept; it would not take food from any hand save hers;
and would not allow any one else to caress it. At the
death of his mistress, the poor cat was removed from
her chamber, but it made its way there the next morning, went on the bed, sat upon her chair, slowly and
mournfully paced over her toilet, and cried most piteously, as if lamenting his poor mistress. After her
funeral, it was found stretched on her grave, apparently
having died from excess of grief.

250. In the summer of 1800, a physician of Lyons
was requested to inquire into a murder that had been
committed on a woman of that city. He accordingly
went to the residence of the deceased, where he found
her extended lifeless on the floor, and weltering in her
blood. A large white cat was mounted on the cornice
of a cupboard, at the farther end of the apartment,
where he seemed to have taken refuge. He sat motionless, with his eyes fixed on the corpse, and his attitude
and looks expressing horror and affright. The following morning he was found in the same station and
attitude; and when the room was filled with the officers
of justice, neither the clattering of the soldiers' arms, nor

the loud conversation of the company, could in the least degree divert his attention. As soon, however, as the suspected persons were brought in, his eyes glared with increased fury; his hair bristled; he darted into the middle of the apartment, where he stopped for a moment to gaze at them, and then precipitately retreated. The countenances of the assassins were disconcerted; and they now, for the first time during the whole course of the horrid business, felt their atrocious audacity forsake them.

251. A cat had kittens, to which she frequently carried mice and other small animals for food, and among the rest she is supposed to have carried a young rat. The kittens, probably not being hungry, played with it; and when the cat gave suck to them, the rat likewise sucked her. This having been observed by some of the servants, Mr. Greenfield had the kittens and rat brought down stairs, and put on the floor; and in carrying them off, the cat was remarked to convey away the young rat as tenderly as she did any of the kittens. This experiment was repeated as often as any company came to the house, till great numbers had become eye-witnesses of the preternatural affection.

252. A little black spaniel had five puppies, which were considered too many for her to bring up. As, however, the breed was much in request, her mistress was unwilling that any of them should be destroyed, and she asked the cook whether she thought it would be possible to bring a portion of them up by hand before the kitchen fire. In reply, the cook observed that the cat had that day kittened, and that, perhaps, the

puppies might be substituted. The cat made no objection, took to them kindly, and gradually all the kittens were taken away, and the cat nursed the two puppies only. Now, the first curious fact was, that the two puppies nursed by the cat were, in a fortnight, as active, forward, and playful as kittens would have been: they had the use of their legs, barked, and gambolled about; while the other three, nursed by the mother, were whining and rolling about like fat slugs. The cat gave them her tail to play with, and they were always in motion ; they soon ate meat, and, long before the others, they were fit to be removed. This was done, and the cat became very inconsolable. She prowled about the house, and on the second day of tribulation fell in with the little spaniel who was nursing the three other puppies. " Oh," says Puss, putting up her back, "it is you who have stolen my children." " No," replied the spaniel with a snarl; "they are my own flesh and blood." "That won't do," said the cat; "I'll take my affidavit before any justice of the peace that you have my two puppies." Thereupon issue was joined ; that is to say, there was a desperate combat, which ended in the defeat of the spaniel, and in the cat walking off proudly with one of the puppies, which she took to her own bed. Having deposited this one, she returned, fought again, gained another victory, and redeemed another puppy. Now, it is very singular that she should have only taken two, the exact number she had been deprived of.

253. We have at present a cat, who has formed a very warm friendship with a large Newfoundland dog. She is constantly caressing him, advances in all haste to

him when he comes in, with her tail erect, then rubs
her head against him, and purrs delightedly. When he
lies before the kitchen fire, she uses him as a bed,
pulling up and settling his hair with her claws to make
it comfortable. As soon as she has arranged it to her
liking, she lies down and composes herself to sleep,
generally purring till she is no longer awake; and they
often lie thus for an hour at a time. Poor Wallace
bears this rough combing of his locks with the most
patient placidity, turning his head towards her during
the operation, and merely giving her a benevolent look,
or gently licking her.

254. I was on a visit to a friend last summer, who
had a favourite cat and dog, which lived together on
the best possible terms, eating from the same plate,
and sleeping on the same rug. Puss had a young
family while I was at the park, and Pincher paid a
daily visit to the kittens, whose nursery was at the top
of the house. One morning there was a tremendous
storm of thunder and lightning; Pincher was in the
drawing-room, and the cat was attending her family
in the garret. Pincher seemed to be considerably
annoyed by the vivid flashes of lightning which con-
tinually startled him, and just as he had crept close
to my feet, some one entered the drawing-room,
followed by puss, who walked in with a disturbed air,
and mewing with all her might. She came up to
Pincher, rubbed her face against his cheek, touched
him gently with her paw, and then walked to the door;
stopped, looked back, mewed—all of which said, as
plainly as words could have done, " Come with me,

Pincher;" but Pincher was too much frightened himself to give any consolation to her, and took no notice
of the invitation. The cat then returned and renewed
her application with increased energy, but the dog was
immoveable, though it was evident that he understood
her meaning, for he turned away his head with a half-
conscious look, and crept still closer to me; and puss
finding all her entreaties unavailing, then left the room.
Soon after this, her mewing became so piteous that I
could no longer resist going to see what was the matter.
I met the cat at the top of the stairs, close to the door
of my sleeping apartment. She ran to me, rubbed
herself against me, and then went into the room, and
crept under the wardrobe. I then heard two voices,
and discovered that she had brought down one of her
kittens, and lodged it there for safety; but her fears
and cares being so divided between the kittens above,
and this little one below, I suppose she wanted Pincher
to watch by this one while she went for the others, for
having confided it to my protection, she hastened up
stairs. I followed her with my young charge, placed it
beside her, and moved their little bed farther from the
window, through which the lightning had flashed so
vividly as to alarm poor puss for the safety of her
family. I remained there till the storm had subsided,
and all was again calm. On the following morning,
much to my surprise, I found her waiting for me at the
door of my apartment. She accompanied me down to
breakfast, sat by me, and caressed me in every possible
way. She had always been in the habit of going down
to breakfast with the lady of the house, but on this

P

morning she had resisted all her coaxing to leave my
door, and would not move a step till I made my
appearance. She went to the breakfast-room with me,
and remained, as I have mentioned, until breakfast
was over, and then went up stairs to her family. She
had never done this before, and never did it again : she
had shown her gratitude for my care of her little ones,
and her duty was done.

255. A cat who had a numerous brood of kittens, one
sunny day in spring encouraged her little ones to
frolic in the vernal beams of noon about the stable-
door, While she was joining them in a thousand
sportive tricks and gambols, they were discovered by a
large hawk, who was sailing above the barn-yard in
expectation of prey. In a moment, swift as lightning,
the hawk darted upon one of the kittens, and had as
quickly borne it off but for the courageous mother, who,
seeing the danger of her offspring, flew on the common
enemy, who, to defend itself, let fall the prize. The battle
presently became seemingly dreadful to both parties;
for the hawk, by the power of his wings, the sharpness
of his talons, and the keenness of his beak, had for
awhile the advantage, cruelly lacerating the poor cat,
and had actually deprived her of one eye in the
conflict; but puss, no way daunted by this accident,
strove with all her cunning and agility for her little
ones, till she had broken the wing of her adversary.
In this state she got him more within the power of
her claws, the hawk still defending himself apparently
with additional vigour; and the fight continued with
equal fury on the side of grimalkin, to the great

entertainment of many spectators. At length victory
seemed to favour the nearly exhausted mother, and she
availed herself of the advantage; for by instantaneous
exertion she laid the hawk motionless beneath her
feet, and, as if exulting in the victory, tore off the head
of the vanquished tyrant. Disregarding the loss of
her eye, she immediately ran to the bleeding kitten,
licked the wounds inflicted by the hawk's talons on its
tender sides, purring while she caressed her liberated
offspring with the same maternal affection as if no
danger had assailed them or their affectionate parent.

256. A friend of Dr. Darwin's saw a cat catch a trout,
by darting upon it in deep clear water, at the mill at
Weaford, near Litchfield. The animal belonged to a
Mrs. Stanley, who had frequently seen her catch fish
in the summer, when the mill-pool was drawn so low
that the fish could be seen.

257. A favourite tabby belonging to a shipmaster was
left on shore by accident while his vessel sailed from
the harbour of Aberdour, Fifeshire, which is about half
a mile from the village. The vessel was about a month
absent, and on her return, to the astonishment of the
shipmaster, puss came on board with a fine stout kitten
in her mouth, apparently about three weeks old, and
went directly down into the cabin. Two others of her
young ones were afterwards caught quite wild in a
neighbouring wood, where she must have remained
with them till the return of the vessel. The shipmaster did not allow her again to go on shore,
otherwise it is probable she would have brought the
whole litter on board. What makes this the more

remarkable is, that vessels were daily entering and leaving the harbour, none of which she ever thought of visiting till the one she had left returned.

258. We have a cat who was a very wild character, often committing depredations in the larder, destroying our young pigeons, and making great havoc among the birds. He was considered so lawless, that, after a consultation on what was best to be done, a decree of banishment was issued against him, and he was sent in a thick linen bag to a cottage at about two miles distance, where he was offered shelter, as he was an expert mouser. We thought we should never see Mr. Tibb again, but found ourselves quite mistaken, for late one evening, about three weeks after, he walked into the kitchen, and greeted every one so kindly, that he met with a more favourable reception than his previous conduct could have warranted him in expecting. Whether he has repented of his late misconduct, whether he is conscious that it was the cause of his banishment, or whether he has passed through scenes which have broken his daring spirit, we cannot say ; but all his bad habits are actually conquered, and he is now quite a pattern of domestic propriety.

259. Still more extraordinary is the instance related by a gentleman who removed his establishment from the county of Sligo to near Dublin, a distance of not less than ninety miles. When about to change his residence, he and his children regretted very much being obliged to leave a favourite cat behind them, which had endeared itself to them by its docility and affection. This gentleman had not been many days

settled in his new abode, when one evening, as the
family were sitting chatting after tea, the servant came
in, followed by a cat so precisely like the one left
behind, that all the family repeated his name at once.
The creature testified great joy in his own way'at the
meeting. He was closely examined, and no difference
whatever was discernible between the cat in Sligo and
that now beside them. Still, it was difficult to believe
it was their poor pet; for how could he have travelled
after them, or how could he have found them out?
And yet the exact resemblance, and the satisfaction
which the poor animal evinced as he walked about,
seemingly in all the confidence of being among his
friends, with his tail erect, and purring with pleasure,
left but little doubt upon their minds that this was
indeed their own cat. The gentleman took him upon
his lap, and examining him closely, found that his
claws were actually worn down, which at once convinced him that poor puss had really travelled the
whole of the ninety miles' journey.

260. A friend of mine possessed a cat and a dog,
which, not being able to live together in peace, had
several contentious struggles for the mastery; and in
the end the dog so completely prevailed, that the cat was
driven away and forced to seek shelter elsewhere.
Several months elapsed, during which the dog alone
possessed the house. At length, however, he was
poisoned by a female servant, whose nocturnal visitors
he had too often betrayed, and was soon afterwards
carried out lifeless into the court before the door. The
cat, from a neighbouring roof, was observed to watch

2 P

the motions of several persons who went up to look at him, and when all were retired, he descended and crept with some degree of caution into the place. He soon ventured to approach, and after having frequently patted the dog with his paw, appeared perfectly sensible that his late quarrelsome companion could no more insult him, and from that time he quietly returned to his former residence and habits.

261. A cat frequented a closet, the door of which was fastened by a common iron latch. A window was situated near the door. When the door was shut, the cat gave herself no uneasiness; for so soon as she was tired of her confinement she mounted on the sill of the window, and with her paws dexterously lifted the latch and came out. This practice she continued for years.

262. We might instance cases in which the reasoning process appears to be exhibited; but let the following, related by Dr. Smellie, in which ingenuity of performance was combined with sagacity, suffice.—A cat frequented a closet, the door of which was fastened by a common iron latch; a window was situated near the door: when the door was shut, the cat gave herself no uneasiness, for as soon as she was tired of her confinement she mounted on the sill of the window, and with her paws dexterously lifted the latch and came out. This practice she continued for years. Many instances of the kind are upon record; let one, however, suffice—of a cat, who having been neglected at the regular dinner hour, which was usually announced by the ringing of the bell, would agitate the bell-wire.

263. In a cloister in France, where the hours of meals were announced by the ringing of a bell, a cat was always in attendance as soon as it was heard, that she, too, according to custom, might be fed. One day it happened that Puss was shut up in a room by herself when the bell rang, so she was not able to avail herself of the summons. Some hours after she was let out, and instantly ran to the spot where dinner was always left for her, but no dinner was to be found. In the afternoon the bell was heard ringing at an unusual hour; when the inmates of the cloister came to see what was the cause of it, they found the cat clinging to the bell-rope, and setting it in motion as well as she was able, in order that she might have her dinner served up to her. In this instance the cat must have been in the habit of observing what went forward, and was therefore led to associate the ringing of the bell with the serving up of dinner; and feeling the want of her meal, very naturally applied herself to perform the act which had already preceded its appearance.

264. An Angora cat belonging to the Charter-house of Paris, having observed that the cook always left the kitchen upon the ringing of a certain bell, and thus left the coast clear for his depredations, soon acquired the art of pulling the bell, and during the cook's absence regularly made off with some of the delicacies which were left unprotected. This trick he repeated at intervals for several weeks, till one day he was detected by a person who was placed in wait for the purloiner.

265. There was a lady who lived at Potsdam with her children, one of whom ran a splinter into her

foot, which caused her to scream out most violently. At first her cries were disregarded, and supposed to proceed from crossness; but at length the eldest sister, who had been asleep, was awakened by the screams, and as she was just getting up to quiet the child, she observed a favourite cat, with whom they were wont to play, and who was of a remarkably gentle disposition, leave its seat under the stove, go to the crying girl, and give her such a smart blow on the cheek with one of its paws, as to draw blood. After this the animal walked back with the greatest composure and gravity to its place, as if satisfied with having chastised the child for crying, and with the hope of indulging in a comfortable nap. No doubt it had often seen the child punished for crossness, and as there was no one near to administer correction, puss had determined to take the law into her own hand.

266 A cat having kittened between the tiles and roof of an out-house, at Earley Court, in August 1835, was a short time afterwards accidentally killed, and two out of the three of her kittens were caught in a trap placed there for that purpose; the third, however, remained in its hiding place eluding all attempts to catch it, when to prevent its being starved, as it was too young to feed itself, a sort of platform was fixed against the tiles, and food and milk placed within its reach. It so happened that a brood of chickens was in the habit of attending the spot near the kitten's quarters, who by degrees approached them, at first with great timidity, but at last, bolder grown, it ventured to lie down amongst them, while they were seeking their food, and follow-

ing wherever they went. It was very amusing and
curious to see the kitten soon, instead of following,
leading its forces, consisting of about twenty hens,
chickens, &c., about the grounds, sometimes catching
at their feet, as if going to bite them, and they pecking
at the kitten in return, sometimes hiding behind a
bush, or concealing itself in the shrubs, and springing
unexpectedly in the midst of them purr and rub itself
against their sides. One pullet in particular was an
especial favourite; it accompanied her every day to her
nest, which was under the boards of an out-house, and
would then lie down at a short distance. The person
who first noticed this circumstance was in the habit of
feeding the kitten, and it was therefore less shy with him
than any one else. He had observed it in the position
described without perceiving the pullet, but when he
did, he was induced to watch whether it remained there
after she had left her nest. He at length observed her
fly off and join the other fowls, when the kitten immediately left its place and followed the pullet, setting
up its tail and purring as if much pleased. It however
did not confine itself to one set of chickens only, but
every fresh brood excited its interest, and was more or
less taken under its protection, the parent hen not
appearing the least alarmed.

267. That there is merriment—genuine human-like
merriment, in many of the lower animals, no one can
doubt, who has ever watched the gambols of the kid,
the cat, the kitten, and the monkey. No experiment,
says a recent writer, can be more beautiful than that of
setting a kitten for the first time before a looking-glass ;

the little creature appears surprised and pleased with
the resemblance, and makes several attempts at touching its new acquaintance: and at length, finding its
efforts fruitless, it looks behind the glass, and appears
highly astonished at the absence of the figure. This
certainly evinces a degree of intelligence.

268. Who has not heard of the favourite cat that
watched by the couch of its dying master, and that
when life was extinct, could scarcely be driven from the
room while his corpse remained, and after his inter-
ment, though repeatedly driven and carried from the
church-yard, was seen to return, regardless of cold, and
unmindful of the cravings of hunger.

269. A friend mentions an anecdote about a cat that
they have.—The butter and milk was kept in a press in
the kitchen, which is fastened by a leather; sometimes
the maids found the door open, when they felt sure they
had fastened it, and some of the butter and milk gone;
so they watched, and saw the cat stand upon her hind-
legs, so as to be able to reach the leather, which she
pulled down by her paw, and so opened the door.

270. We had a cat when I was a child, which would
leap up and put her paw on the latch of the door going
from the yard into the kitchen, and so open it. I
remember this quite well.

271. A kitten once attached herself to me in a manner
which was certainly very remarkable, particularly as I
do not remember ever to have cultivated her affections
by any other means than those of simple kindness and
attention.

# THE WOLF.

——◄❉►——

Nature never did betray
The heart that loved her! 'Tis her privilege,
Through all the years of this our life, to lead
From joy to joy, for she can so inform
The mind that is within us, so impress
With quietness and beauty, and so feed
With lofty thoughts, that neither evil tongues,
Rash judgments, nor the sneers of selfish men,
Nor greetings where no kindness is, nor all
The dreary intercourse of common life,
Shall e'er prevail against us, or disturb
Our cheerful faith that all that we behold
Is full of blessings,—WORDSWORTH.

272. A very interesting account is given of the attachment which a wolf exhibited, even in the hour of
death. A large tame wolf, caught at Aspro, and brought
up from a cub on ship-board, was exceedingly docile.
He was a favourite with the whole crew, but he was
particularly attached to the lieutenant. A violent
storm came on, and it was evident the ship must be
lost. The animal was sensible of the danger. His
howls were peculiarly distressing, and he would not be
driven from the side of his friend. On the breaking
up of the ship, both of them got upon the mast.
Sometimes one of ·them was washed off, and sometimes
the other; but by the eager assistance which they

rendered each other, they again ãnd again recovered
their hold.    At length the lieutenant exhausted by
continual exertion, was almost benumbed.   The wolf
was equally fatigued; aud it was partly by clinging to
each other and to the mast that they were enabled to
keep themselves from being washed away.   The mast
drifted towards the shore, and was at no great distance
from it, when the lieutenant, totally unable to support
himself any longer, and remembering the attachment
of the animal, even in death, turned towards him from
the mast.   The beast clapped his fore-paws round his
neck, while the lieutenant clasped him in his arms,
and they sunk together.

# THE SHEEP.

——•¦ ✖ ¦•+——

Nature, enchanting Nature, in whose form
And lineaments divine I trace a hand
That errs not, and find raptures still renew'd,
Is free to all men—universal prize.
Strange that so fair a creature should yet want
Admirers, and be destined to divide
With meaner objects ee'n the few she finds !—COWPER.

273. Amongst other instances of sagacity in sheep, I have often been amused by the perfect knowledge which they have of the boundaries of the farm to which they belong. From being frequently driven back when found wandering, they soon learn the exact boundary lines within which they are left in peace both by the shepherd and his dog.

274. In December, 1825, Thomas Rae, blacksmith, Hardhills, parish of Brittle, purchased a lamb of the black-faced breed from an individual passing with a large flock. It was so extremely wild, that it was with great difficulty separated from its fleecy companions. He put it into his field in company with a cow and a little white galloway. It never seemed to mind the cow, but soon exhibited manifest indications of fondness for the pony, which, not insensible to such tender approaches, amply demonstrated the attachment to be

reciprocal. They were now to be seen in company in all circumstances, whether the pony was used for riding or drawing. Such a spectacle no doubt drew forth the officious gaze of many; and when likely to be too closely beset, the lamb would seek an asylum beneath the pony, and pop out its head betwixt the fore or hind legs, with looks of conscious security. At night, it invariably repaired to the stable, and reposed under the manger, before the head of its favourite. When separate, which only happened when effected by force, the lamb would raise the most plaintive bleatings and the pony a responsive neighing. On one occasion they both strayed into an adjoining field, in which was a flock of sheep; the lamb joined the flock at a short distance from the pony, but as soon as the owner removed him, it quickly followed without the least regard to its own species. Another instance of the same description happened when riding through a large flock; it followed on without showing any symptoms of a wish to remain with its natural companions.

# THE MOUSE.

———•**t 祝 }**•+———

Thy desire, which tends to know
The works of God, thereby to glorify
The great Workmaster, leads to no excess
That reaches blame, but rather merits praise—
The more it seems excess.—MILTON.

275. A SIMILAR action to that of the fox has been observed in a little animal to which it is not common to
ascribe more than an ordinary degree of cunning or
confidence in its own resources. In a book-case of
wainscot, impervious to light, different articles were
kept which were more agreeable to the taste of mice
than books, when, at midday, the doors were suddenly
opened, a mouse was seen on one of the shelves, and
so rivited was the little creature to the spot, that it
showed all the signs of death, not moving a limb when
taken into the hand On another occasion, on opening
a parlour door in broad daylight, a mouse was seen fixed
and motionless in the middle of the room, and on
advancing towards it, its appearance in no way differed
from that of a dead animal, excepting that it had not
fallen over on its side. Neither of these creatures made
an effort to escape, and were taken up at leisure; nor
had they received any hurt or injury, for they soon displayed every mark of being alive and well.

# THE BADGER.

—••❘✖❘•••—

With wise intent
The hand of Nature on peculiar minds
Imprints a different bias, and to each
Decrees its province in the common toil—AKENSIDE.

276. As two persons passed through a hollow way,
their dog started and killed a badger. Being only a
little way from the village, they agreed to drag him
there, as the commune gave a reward for every one that
was destroyed. They twisted some twigs, and drew
him along the road by turns. They had not proceeded
far, when they heard the cry of an animal in seeming
distress, and, stopping to see whence it proceeded,
another badger was approaching. They endeavoured
to drive it away with stones, but it would not be repulsed; it came close to the dead animal, and began to
lick it, and continued its mournful cry. The men had
it not in their hearts any longer to repulse him, but
they continued to draw the dead one along. The other
laid himself down upon his dead companion, clasping it
closely, and was thus drawn into the village, where, to
the shame of its inhabitants, it was speedily destroyed.

# THE RAVEN.

———•!✳!•·——

In nature there is nothing melancholy.—COLERIDGE.

277. Mr. THOMPSON, in his Natural History of Ireland, gives the following:—It was a common practice in a spacious yard at Belfast, to lay trains of corn for sparrows, and then to shoot them from a window, only so far open as to afford room for the muzzle of the gun; neither the instrument of destruction nor the shooter being visible from the outside. A tame raven, which was a nestling when brought to the yard, and probably had never seen a shot fired, afforded evidence that it understood the whole affair. When any one appeared carrying a gun across the yard towards the house from which the sparrows were fired at, the raven exhibited the utmost alarm, by hurrying off with all possible speed, but a ludicrously awkward gait, to hide itself, screaming loudly all the while. Though alarmed for its own safety, this bird always concealed itself near to and within view of the field of action; the shot was hardly fired, when it darted out from its retreat, and seizing one of the dead or wounded sparrows, hurried back to his hiding-place. I have often witnessed the whole scene. And again, the following communicated to him by Mr. R. Ball:—When a boy at school, a tame raven

Q

was very attentive in watching our cribs or bird traps; and when a bird was taken, he endeavoured to catch it by turning up the crib, but in so doing the bird always escaped, as the raven could not let go the crib in time to seize it. After several vain attempts of this kind, the raven, seeing another bird caught, instead of going at once to the crib, went to another tame raven, and induced it to accompany him, when the one lifted up the crib, and the other bore the poor captive off in triumph.

278. Another after eating its fill, used to conceal the remaining pieces of food under several loose stones which were close to the shed, and when hungry, repeatedly have I and other boys watched him going straight to the place where he concealed his first morsel, and so on to the last stone in rotation.

279. Lord Bacon, it is said, gives an account of a raven that filled up with pebbles some hollow in a tree containing water, in order to make the liquid rise up to a point within its reach. Lord Brougham brings it under the head of animal intelligence.

# THE PIGEON.

——◆❀◆——

Deep in the wood thy voice I list, and love
Thy soft complaining song--thy tender cooing;
Oh! what a winning way thou hast of wooing!
Gentlest of all thy race—sweet turtle dove.

280. EVERY sportsman knows that the common wood
pigeon, (the Ring Dove,) is one of the shyest birds we
have, and so wild, that it is very difficult indeed to get
within shot of one. This wild bird has however been
known to lay aside its usual habits. In the spring of
1839, some village boys brought two young wood pigeons
taken from the nest, to the parsonage-house of a clergyman in Gloucestershire, from whom I received the
following anecdote :—They were bought from the boys
merely to save their lives, and sent to an old woman
near the parsonage to be bred up. She took great care
of them, feeding them with peas, of which they are
very fond. One of them died, but the other grew up,
and was a fine bird. Its wings had not been cut, and
as soon as it could fly, it was set at liberty. Such, however, was the effect of the kindness it had received, that
it would never quite leave the place. It would fly to
great distances, and even associate with others of its
own kind ; but it never failed to come to the house
twice a day to be fed. The peas were placed for it on

the kitchen window. If the window was shut, it would tap with its beak till it was opened, then come in, eat its meal, and then fly off again. If by any accident it could not gain admittance, it would wait somewhere till the cook came out, when it would pitch on her shoulder, and go with her into the kitchen. What made this more extraordinary was, that the cook had not bred the bird up, and the old woman's cottage was at a little dis· tance; but as she had no peas left, it came to the parsonage to be fed. This went on for some time; but the poor bird having lost its fear of man, was therefore exposed to constant danger from those who did not know it. It experienced the fate of most pets;—a stran ger saw it quietly sitting on a tree, and shot it, to the great regret of all its former friends."

# THE PARTRIDGE.

Wonderful indeed are all His works, all
Pleasant to know, and worthiest to be had
In remembrance always with delight.—MILTON.

281. THE following remarkable anecdote may not be considered out of place here, although it is not improbable that in this instance the bird was actuated simply by στοργι.—A partridge, which had her nest in a hedgerow close to a footpath leading to a farm house, in the Isle of Wight, sat there upon thirteen eggs, and appeared so little disturbed by the presence of the passers by, that the farmer one day, from curiosity, put his hand down to see if she would permit him to touch her. The bird however flew off, but, doing so hastily, became caught in the briars surrounding the nest, and he took her up. He then perceived that her crop had been ripped up by a thorn, and to such an extent that its contents escaped through the rent. He took the bird into the house, where his wife, with the assistance of her maid, carefully sewed up, one after another, the wounds in the inner and outer skins of the crop, rubbed in a little salt butter by way of a salve, and set the bird at liberty. Away she flew; but within a very short time, in spite of all that had occurred, she had actually

returned to her eggs, of which, in due time, she succeeded in hatching twelve.

282. A hen partridge has been known, on perceiving
that her nest was discovered, to cover the eggs over
with leaves so completely, that it (the nest) could not
have been casually noticed; and each morning as she
laid a fresh egg, she covered all over again. Indeed the
nest is always most carefully concealed and covered
with the surrounding herbage, and care is taken not to
leave any trace to or from it. Montagu mentions one
which, being taken with her eggs, continued to sit on
them, and brought out the young. He gives an instance
of a partridge being taken away with her eggs, in a hat,
in which she continued to sit, and *hatch*ed them, suit-
ing the action to the word.

283. Mr. Jesse relates a curious anecdote of a partridge
which, being disturbed by a plough driven close to her
nest, removed the eggs, nineteen in number, assisted
perhaps by her mate, to a distance of forty yards, under
a hedge, before the return of the plough, an interval of
twenty minutes; such instances have more than once
occurred. Of another he says,—A farmer discovered
a partridge sitting on its eggs in a grass field. The
bird allowed him to pass his hand down its back without moving or shewing any fear; but if he offered to
touch the eggs, the poor bird immediately pecked his
hand. Another has been known to fly at and attack a
person who picked up one of her young in a road, on
hearing its cry.

# THE SEA GULL.

———

Sounds inharmonious in themselves and harsh,
Yet heard in scenes where peace for ever reigns,
And only there, please highly for their sake.—Cowper.

284. I have known of two instances in which gulls, which had been caught young, and tamed, have continued to keep up their intimacy with those who reared them, after they had gained the full use of their wings, and were at perfect liberty; though they took advantage of it to go away every year at the breeding season, and might have been supposed to have entirely resumed their natural habits. Both of these instances occurred in the Isle of Wight—one at Calbourne, where I well remember " Old Phil," as he was called, year after year, sailing over the village green, and alighting on a low wall at the grocer's shop, from which he used to be fed with bits of cheese, of which he was very fond, and other dainties. The other instance was near Sea View, where, I am informed, the gull used to return in the same way, his former tameness not appearing to have been at all affected by his temporary retirement into wild life. Not the least remarkable part of the history of these birds is that, during the breeding season, each of them occasionally brought his mate with him to introduce her to his old friends, and to invite her to partake of their hospitality.

I dont think indeed, that "Old Phil" ever prevailed on
his better-half to come and share his cheese, but she
used to keep him company into the village, and sometimes amuse herself in a pond hard by, whilst he went
to pay his accustomed visit to the grocer. In the other
case, near Sea View, my informant tells me the wild
gull used to come up and feed with the tame one under
his dining-room windows, though she would not approach quite close as long as any one was visible at
them, but sat on the grass plat a short distance off, or
hovered round until the coast seemed clear. Perhaps
there is naturally less fear of man entertained by gulls
than by most other birds. One can scarcely be for a
few hours at sea, or by the water in a harbour town,
without some of them, from curiosity or carelessness,
coming round so close to one as to afford sufficient
proof of this. Last year, (1858,) whilst fishing at some
distance outside the harbour at Stornoway, I threw
over, foul-hooked, and brought into the boat, with a
short cuddy rod and line, two gulls, as they flew round
close to us, allured by the hope of a share in our fish.
The first, when released, not having exhibited the
slightest fear, but continued to hover round us, closer,
if anything, than before, as if he fancied he had then a
special claim to our attention, I thought, on catching
the second, I would see to what extent he might be
disposed to entertain friendly relations towards us.
Accordingly I took him in my lap, and offered him some
nice bits of fish. At first he professed to be angry and
pecked at my fingers instead of the fish, as if to ask
whether I thought it possible that he would condescend

to accept my donations under restraint. However, having accidentally-on-purpose got hold of a piece of fish, down it went; and, apparently thinking that under the circumstances he might do worse, he set to work with no ill will or appetite, and soon got through a good part of a haddock. On regaining his liberty, so far from appearing to resent my compulsory kindness, he rather seemed to wish for a repetition of the same course of treatment, for he continued to fly backwards and forwards within a few feet of our heads, as if he thought he had been a fool after all. The captain of one of the Dover and Ostend steamers told me that he had seen a gull come and take off the taffrail food which had been placed there for him.

285. They are naturally fearless birds, and far from shy, and are readily kept in confinement. A gull, which lived for twenty-seven years, used to go away in summer, and pair with another of the wild birds, in the cliffs of the Isle of Wight, returning alone afterwards, and spending its time either on a small piece of water, or sitting on the railings of some cottage, or else flying about the country, so tame withal, that it would come into the houses and eat from the hands of persons whom it knew, though not from others.

# THE NIGHTINGALE.

All is still;
A balmy night! and though the stars be dim,
Yet let us think upon the vernal shower
That gladdens the green earth, and we shall find
A pleasure in the dimness of the stars:
And hark! the Nightingale begins its song.—COLERIDGE.


286. THE late Bishop Stanley relates the following
account of one which was reared from the nest in the
spring of 1835:— It soon became tame, and was kept
in a cage till May 1837, singing always in the winter
from Christmas till April, and showing no symptoms of
impatience at the usual period of migration; it was
silent the rest of the year. Last May it was permitted
to go out of its cage, which was hung up open, at the
door of the office. At first it returned regularly in the
evening to its cage, and was taken in, and released
again the next morning. As the season advanced, it
sometimes stayed out all night in the shrubberies and
pleasure-grounds, but if called by any one of the servants, whose voice it knew, would return and feed out
of their hand. For a day or two, towards the close of
the summer, it seemed rather uneasy, but this soon wore
off. As the evenings got cool in the autumn, it returned
to its cage before nightfall, and was taken as usual into

the house ; as the season still further advanced, it was permanently housed, and was expected to sing again at Christmas.

287. He also mentions a remarkable instance of their removing their eggs, under peculiar circumstances, as communicated to the French Academy of Sciences, by M. Merveaux —A pair of these birds had built their nest in his garden, in the lower part of a hedge, containing four eggs, when some water in the neighbourhood rose with such impetuosity as to inundate the garden. He watched them with some anxiety; and one day when the water had reached to within six paces of the nest, he only perceived two eggs. He at first thought that the nest had been abandoned; but coming to it very soon after, he only saw one, and this time he waited to see the result, and was much astonished to see the last egg disappear with the birds, who, flying cautiously, but rapidly, carried it to a new nest, at the highest part of the hedge, where he saw all the four eggs deposited in safety, and where they were afterwards hatched.

288. The attachment of this species to its young, and its grief at their loss, have been noticed by many writers, ancient and modern. Our friend, the Rev. E. G. Moor, sends us, on this subject, a memorandum from his journal:—One evening, while I was at College, he says, happening to drink tea with the late Rev. J. Lambert, fellow of Trinity College, he told me the following fact, illustrative of Virgil's extreme accuracy in describing natural objects. We had been speaking of those well-known lovely lines in the fourth Georgic on the Nightingale's lamentation for the loss of her

young, when Mr. Lambert told me that riding once through one of the toll gates near Cambridge, he observed the keeper of the gate and his wife, who were aged persons, apparently much dejected. Upon inquiring into the cause of their uneasiness, the man assured Mr. Lambert that he and his wife had both been made very unhappy by a nightingale, which had built in their garden, and had the day before been robbed of its young. This loss she had been deploring in such a melancholy strain all the night, as not only to deprive him and his wife of sleep, but also to leave them in the morning full of sorrow; from which they had evidently not recovered when Mr. Lambert saw them.

# THE PARROT.

——◦ ⁙ ◦——

Thus Nature works as if to mock at Art,
And in defiance of her rival power,
By these fortuitous and random strokes
Performing such inimitable feats
As she with all her wiles could never reach.

289. In a pleasant article contributed to Fraser's
Magazine, in October, 1857, entitled "Jays and Nutcrackers," are collected some anecdotes of birds, with
a view of proving that those brought up in confinement,
and taught to speak, in time become acquainted with
the meaning of the words which they utter. Now
whether such cases as those referred to are merely the
result of accidental coincidence; whether having been
taught to associate certain words with certain actions,
it is only by rote, and mechanically, that birds are led
to repeat them at the appropriate times, as they un-
questionably do; or whether they really ever understand the meaning of what they say, it would be hard
to prove, no matter to what extent instances might be
multiplied. Although I confess I do not give birds
credit for so much sense as the author of "Jays and
Nutcrackers," yet I will contribute an anecdote, for the
accuracy of which I can vouch, and which, so far as it
goes, certainly tends to prove his theory. A parrot

belonging to some friends of mine, was generally taken out of the room when the family assembled for prayers, for fear lest he might take it into his head to join irreverently in the responses. One evening, however, his presence happened to be unnoticed, and he was forgotten. For some time he maintained a decorous silence, but at length, instead of " Amen," out he came with " Cheer boys, cheer." On this, the butler was directed to remove him, and had got as far as the door with him, when the bird, perhaps thinking that he had committed himself, and had better apologize, called out, " Sorry I spoke." The overpowering effect on the congregation may be more easily imagined than described.

290. The parrot of a relation of mine also used, whenever he dropped anything he was eating, to say, " Pick up baby's crust," being doubtless prompted by the same train of associations as those which lead another parrot, which I know well, invariably to say, " Thank you," whenever anything is given to him.

291. The following story is not a bad one, but all that I can say with regard to its authenticity is, si non è vero, è ben trovato :—If it be not true, it deserves to be so, for the sake of both master and pupil. Some parrot fanciers had agreed to meet in a year's time, when each was to shew a bird for a prize, proficiency in talking being by common consent to be the great criterion of merit. On the day appointed, all the rest came, each duly bringing his parrot; one only appeared without his. On being asked why he had not shown one according to the agreement, he said that he had tried to train one, but that he was such a stupid bird he was quite

ashamed to bring him. The excuse was held to be inadmissible. All the others insisted that, stupid or clever, he must be produced, and his master accordingly went off for and returned with him. No sooner was he introduced, than, looking round at the large assemblage of birds, he exclaimed, " What a lot of Parrots !" The prize was immediately voted to him by acclamation.

292. The following story has often been recorded before, but it will bear repeating :—A tradesman who had a shop in the Old Bailey, London, opposite the prison, bought two parrots, a green and a grey. The green parrot was taught to speak when there was a knock at the street door ; the grey, whenever the bell rang ; but they only knew two short phrases of English. The house in which they lived had an old-fashioned, projecting front, so that the first-floor could not be seen from the pavement ; and, on one occasion, they were left outside the window by themselves, when some one knocked at the street door. " Who is there ?" said the green parrot. " The man with the leather," was the reply, to which the bird answered, " Oh ! oh !" The door, not being opened, the stranger knocked a second time. " Who is there ?" said green poll. " Who is there ?" exclaimed the man ; " Why don't you come down ?" " Oh ! oh !" repeated the parrot. This so enraged the stranger, that he rang the bell furiously. " Go to the gate," said a new voice, which belonged to the grey parrot. " To the gate ?" repeated the man, who saw no such entrance, and who thought that the servants were bantering him " What gate ?" he asked,

stepping back to view the premises. " New-gate," responded the grey, just as the angry applicant discovered
who had been answering his summonses. Parrots have
been known to mimic the sound of planing a deal
board, the mewing of a cat, or the barking of a dog, so
accurately as to deceive the closest observers.

293. The predilection of animals for particular persons, was once the means of deciding, very amusingly,
a case before a court of justice. It was at a Dublin
police-office, and the object of dispute was a pet parrot,
which had been stolen from a Mr Davis, and sold to a
Mr. Moore. The plaintiff, taking the bird upon his
finger, said, " Come, old boy, give me a kiss," which the
parrot instantly did. A youth, in the defendant's interest, remarked that this proved nothing, as the parrot
would kiss anybody  " You had better not try," remarked the plaintiff. Nevertheless, the young man
asked the parrot to kiss him. Poll, advanced as if to
give the required salute, but seized the youth's lip, and
made him roar with pain. This fact, and the parrot's
obeying the plaintiff, in several other requisitions,
caused it to be instantly ordered into the possession of
its original master.

294. A parallel case to that of the geese who saved the
capitol of Rome, has happened at Camden, New Jersey.
It appears that Mr. John Hutchinson has a very loqua-
cious parrot, as well as a well-stocked plate chest. One
day, some greedy New Jerseymen resolved to try the
virtue of silver forks at their own dinner-table, and consequently broke into the pantry. As they were just on

the point of securing the plate, they heard a loud and awful voice exclaim, " You lazy rascals, I see you! John, bring my revolver!" They made one rush for the window, which they had forced open, and in their trepidation got into the yard of a neighbour, who had a fierce dog. A great noise was the result, and the police awakening, one of the three men was captured. The parrot had saved the plate.

# THE WHITETHROAT.

1—◦•✦✖✦•◦—

Song-birds of Nature, ye whose bursting throats
People the wild-wood with your mellow notes,
I love ye all!        G. J. O. ALLMAN.

295. I REMEMBER finding, when a boy, the nest of a
whitethroat, which she had constructed in the stem of
a tall hemlock. Whilst engaged in the work of incuba-
tion, she appeared to be perfectly devoid of fear, and
would not only permit my sister and my self to stroke
her on her nest, but would actually take food from our
hands, thus proving that her tameness was not merely
the result of that mysterious στοϱγη—that love for her
young, which in the female seems to annihilate all sense
of fear, but that, apart from it, she had lost that dread
of man by which she would at other times have been
more or less influenced.

# THE LANDRAIL.

——•✠❉✠•——

Winter is past
And the stormy blast
Is hastening away to the northward at last.

296. THE following well-told relation of the fact it
records, I give as communicated to me by William Robert
Shepherd, Esq., of the Dana, Shrewsbury :—Rather a
singular circumstance occurred to me the other day.
Whilst out with my gun on the 13th instant, at Ludlow,
in this county, in going over a grass field, my dog in
advance flushed a Corn-Crake, which fled steadily for a
short distance and then dropped among the grass.
Being desirous of watching its movements, I hurried to
the spot where it had alighted, where I saw it stealing
through the grass with the stealthiness and rapidity of
a mouse, ever and anon raising its head to see the extent
of the danger.   I was thus watching it, when suddenly
it stopped and crouched close to the ground.   Motion-
ing the dog to stay behind, I crept cautiously to the
spot, and as I drew near to it, was surprised to see no
attempt at escape.   Having reached the place, I carefully examined the ground for some distance round, but
could find nothing.   I was just on the point of giving
up the search, thinking that the bird had stolen off

without my notice, when my attention was attracted by
what appeared to me to be a clod of earth lying on
the ground among the grass. I walked to it, and on
stooping down, was no less surprised than pleased to
find the object of my search apparently lifeless. I took
it up—the head and legs dropped; to all appearance
the bird was quite dead. Being well acquainted with the
habits of birds, I immediately detected the imposition;
so placing the bird upon the ground, I retired to a short
distance under cover of the trunk of a large tree. I
had not remained long before I saw the cunning bird
gently move, when suddenly starting to its legs, it ran a
short distance; then taking wing, soon disappeared
over an adjoining hedge. This is a striking instance
of that deep cunning and sagacity which characterizes
the habits of some birds; as such, I have thought it
worth recording.

297. Mr. Jesse has given a similar account in his
"Gleanings in Natural History," as follows:—A gentleman had a Corn-Crake brought to him by his dog,
to all appearance quite dead. As it lay on the ground,
he turned it over with his foot, and was convinced that
it was dead. Standing by, however, in silence, he suddenly saw it open one eye; he then took it up, its head
fell, its legs hung, and it appeared again quite dead.
He then put it in his pocket, and before long he felt it
all alive, and struggling to escape. · He then took it out;
it was as lifeless as before. Having laid it again upon
the ground, and retired to some distance, the bird, in
about five minutes, warily raised its head, looked round,
and decamped at full speed.

# THE BLACKBIRD.

———•‡✕‡•———

Cheered and chastened
Onward I hastened
Blessing the bird for its merry song,
It haunted my heart the whole day long.—THOMAS HOOD.

298. A VERY young blackbird, says Mr. Jesse, was
put into a cage, which was hung up under the porch of
a lodge ; after the bird had begun to feed, an older
blackbird was caught and put into the same cage. This
old bird moped, and refused to feed itself, and would
probably have died, had not the younger brought it food
in its bill, and in every respect treated it as if it had
been its mother, nourishing it with the greatest perseverance for some time. Again, a cat was observed on
the top of a paled fence, endeavouring to get at a blackbird's nest which was near it; the hen left the nest on
her approach, flew to meet her in a state of great alarm,
and placed herself almost within her reach, uttering the
most piteous screams of wildness and despair. The
cock bird, on perceiving the danger, showed the greatest
distress, and uttered loud screams and outcries, sometimes settling on the fence just before the cat, who was
unable to make a spring, in consequence of the narrow-
ness of its footing. After a little time, the cock bird
flew at the cat, settled on her back, and pecked her
R

head with such violence that she fell to the ground, followed by the blackbird, who succeeded in driving her away. A second time the same scene occurred; the blackbird was again victorious, and the cat became so intimidated at the attacks made upon her, that she gave over her attempts to get at the young ones. After each battle the blackbird celebrated his victory with a song, and for several days afterwards he would hunt the cat about the garden whenever she left the house. He adds that he also knew an instance of a pair of blackbirds following a boy into a house, and pecking at his head while he was conveying one of their young into it. He very properly observes that people little think what misery they occasion to birds when they deprive them of the brood which they have been cherishing with so much tenderness and affection. " The cruel parent, says an old author, " that would encourage his childe to deprive a poor birde of her broode, right well deserveth to have his own nest robbed, and to become childless."

# THE THRUSH.

——•ː¦¢ ¦•·——

If thou art pain'd with this world's noisy stir,
And crazed with its mad tumults, and weighed down
With any of the ills of human life ;
If thou art sick and weak, or mourn'st the loss
Of brethren gone to that far-distant land
To which we all do pass, gentle and poor,
The gayest and the gravest, all alike —
Then turn into the peaceful woods, and hear
The thrilling music of the forest birds.—J. McLELLAN, JUN.

299. A SHORT time ago, in Scotland, some carpenters working in a shed adjacent to a house, observed one of these birds flying in and out, which induced them to direct their attention to the cause, when to their surprise, they found a nest commenced among the teeth of a harrow, which, with some other farming-tools and implements, were placed upon the joists of the shed just over their heads. The carpenters had arrived soon after six o'clock; and at seven, when they found the nest, it was in a state of great forwardness, and had evidently been the morning's work of a pair of these indefatigable birds. Their activity throughout the day was incessant, and when the workmen left off in the evening, and came again in the morning, they found the female seated on her half-finished mansion ; and when she flew off for a short time, it was discovered that

she had already laid an egg, though the bottom of the nest was the only part plastered and completed. When all was finished, the male bird took his share in the hatching, and though he did not sit so long, he was very attentive in feeding her when on the nest: the young were hatched in thirteen days. As they grew, and required greater supplies, the entrance and retreat of the old ones through the door was so rapid that it could scarcely be seen, but was only known by the sound as they darted over the heads of the men— another proof of the rapidity of flight of even the slower flying birds, when urged by necessity,

# THE STORK.

Go with me if you like, upon report.—As You Like It.

300. A FRENCH Surgeon at Smyrna, wishing to procure a stork, and finding great difficulty, on account of
the extreme veneration in which they are held by the
Turks, stole all the eggs out of a nest and replaced them
with those of a hen. In process of time the young
chickens came forth, much to the astonishment of the
storks. In a short time the male went off, and was not
seen for two or three days, when he returned with an
immense crowd of his companions, who all assembled
in the place, and formed a circle, taking no notice of the
numerous spectators, which so unusual an occurrence
had collected. The female was brought forward into
the midst of the circle, and after some consultation, the
whole flock fell upon her, and tore her to pieces; after
which they immediately dispersed, and the nest was
entirely abandoned.

301. The following in many respects, similar case,
occurred on the estate of a gentleman of large landed
property near Berlin, and is a valuable corroboration of
what might, to many, appear as unworthy of credit. A
pair of Storks built a nest on one of the chimneys of
his mansion; having a curiosity to inspect it, the

2 R

owner climbed up, and found in it one egg, which being about the size of a goose's egg, was replaced by one belonging to that bird. The storks seemed not to notice the exchange, but no sooner was the egg hatched, than the male bird perceiving the difference, rose from the nest, and flying round it several times with loud screams, disappeared, and was not seen again for three days, during which time the female continued to tend her offspring as usual. Early on the fourth morning, however, the inmates of the house were disturbed by loud and discordant cries in the field fronting the house, when they perceived about five hundred storks assembled in a dense body, and one standing about twenty yards before the rest, apparently haranguing its companions, who stood listening, to all appearance, with great emotion. When this bird had concluded, it retired and another took its place, and seemed to address them in a similar manner. This proceeding and noise was repeated by several successive birds, until about eleven o'clock in the forenoon, when the whole flock simultaneously arose in the air uttering dismal cries. The female all this time was observed to remain on her nest, watching their motions with apparent trepidation. In a short time the body of storks made towards her, headed by one bird, supposed to be the male, who struck her vehemently three or four times, and knocked her out of the nest; the whole mass then followed the attack, until they had not only destroyed the female stork, (who made no attempt either to escape or defend herself,) but the young gosling, and utterly removed every vestige of the nest itself. Since that time about four years ago, no stork has been known to build there.

302 Some hen's eggs were placed in a stork's nest, and the others removed. The female stork, not aware of the change, sat patiently the appointed number of days, till the shells were broken, and the young chickens made their appearance. No sooner were they seen by the old birds, then they testified their surprise by harsh notes and fierce looks, and after a short pause, they jointly fell upon the unfortunate chickens and pecked them to pieces, as if conscious of the disgrace which might be supposed to attach to a dishonoured nest.

# THE SWAN.

—•✠•—

The love of nature's works
· Is an ingredient in the compound man,
Infus'd at the creation of the kind.
And, though the Almighty Maker has throughout
Discriminated each from each by strokes
And touches of his hand, with so much art
Diversified, that two were never found
Twins at all points—yet this obtains in all,
That all discern a beauty in his works,
And all can taste them : minds that have been formed
And tutored, with a relish more exact,
But none without some relish,—none unmoved.—COWPER.

303. On the Thames last summer I was amused by
watching an old swan feeding her young ones, in what
seemed to me a novel and ingenious manner. Sitting
on the water with her breast against the bank, she
gathered from it the grass as far over as she could
reach, and then, turning round her long neck, threw it
over her back to the cygnets, who seemed quite up to
the manœuvre and were waiting and scrambling for it
in the water behind her. My attention was called to it
by the fisherman who was with me, and who,—though
he had lived all his life by the banks of the Thames—
said he had never witnessed this before.

# THE OWL.

———✦❊✦✦——

Sweet the coming on
Of grateful evening mild; then silent night
With this her bird, and this fair moon,
And these the gems of heaven, the starry train.—MILTON.

304. WHITE has mentioned a tame barn-owl with which
he was acquainted. A friend of mine has sent me the
following particulars respecting a tame white one, which
was taken when young, from a nest in the wood at
Dilstone, near Hexham in Northumberland, and given
by a lady to her children, who brought it up. Great
pains appear to have been taken to domesticate this
owl, in consequence of which it became familiar. In
imitation of its own call, it received the name of *Keevie*,
to which it would readily answer when within hearing,
following the sound from whatever part of the premises
it might happen to be in. Its usual place of repose
during the day was under the branches of an old Scotch
fir, which grew down a steep inaccessible bank, where
it would sit apparently asleep, but sufficiently awake to
endeavour to attract the notice of any one who passed
by its usual cry of *keevi , keevie.* If the passenger
stopped and answered it, it immediately scrambled up
the boughs of the fir, till it brought itself to a level with
the walk above, in hope of being fed; but if he went

on again, unheeding its solicitations, it returned to its
former place, and resumed its slumbers. One of the
most striking peculiarities in this tame owl is said to
have been its fondness for music. It would often come
into the drawing-room of an evening, on the shoulder
of one of the children, and, on hearing the tones of the
piano, would sit with its eyes gravely fixed on the instrument, and its head on one side in an attitude of
attention; when, suddenly spreading its wings, he would
alight on the keys, and making a dart at the performer's
fingers with its beak, would continue hopping about, as
if pleased with the execution. After a while the flight
of this owl into the woods became longer, and he only
returned at dusk to receive his usual supper from the
person who was in the habit of feeding him, and whom
he readily permitted at such times to take him up, and
carry him into the house for this purpose. Bye-and-bye
it was observed that he did not devour his meals in the
kitchen as formerly, but fled along the passage, dragging
the meat after him, till he reached the garden door,
when he flew with it to a part of the shrubbery. On
being followed, it was discovered that he had brought
with him a companion, who, not having courage to
accompany him the whole way, remained at a respectful
distance to receive his bounty. After having served his
visitor in this manner, he returned to the kitchen, and
leisurely devoured his own portion. This practice was
continued for some months, till at length one evening
he was missed, and nowhere to be found; his companion, it is said, continued to visit the spot alone for
several weeks, uttering doleful cries, but could never be

persuaded to come near to be fed. It proved in the end, that the favourite had been killed; and its stuffed skin was one day recognized, alas! in a woodman's hut, by the children who had so assiduously nurtured it and brought it up.

305. A brown owl had long been in the occupation of a convenient hole in a hollow tree, and in it for several years had rejoiced over its progeny, with hope of the pleasure to be enjoyed in excursions of hunting in their company; but, through the persecutions of some persons on the farm, who had watched the bird's proceedings, this hope had been repeatedly disappointed by the plunder of the nest at the time when the young ones were ready for flight. On the last occasion, an individual was ascending to their retreat, to repeat the robbery, when the parent bird, aware of the danger, grasped her only young one in her claws, and bore it away; and never more was the nest placed in the same situation.

306. The following curious account has been forwarded to me by Mr. Chaffey, of Dodington, Kent:—My old owl, a brown one, I had in my possession twenty-six years. When she was about sixteen years old, she laid two eggs, and sat upon them some time before I discovered it. As soon as I did, I took them away, and replaced them with two bantam's eggs, upon which she sat about a fortnight, and then forsook them Last year she again laid two eggs, one of them only having a hard shell, she sat upon the one egg for about a fortnight, when I examined it and found it addled. I then took it away, and procured a hen's egg which had been sat upon about the same time, and which in due time

she hatched. Never in my life did I see any bird half
so tender and careful of their young as she was; for the
first few days she hardly let it have time to feed, taking
it by the neck off my hand, and running with it into
the dark corner where it was hatched. After a short
time it would eat as freely as the old owl. When the
chicken was about three month's old, the poor old owl
choked herself by swallowing part of a fowl which I had
given her for her supper. I had turned the male owl
out as soon as the chicken was hatched. He used to
come every evening to the place and remain there for
hours, till the death of the other bird; after which, I saw
or heard nothing more of him.—The chicken grew up a
very fine bird.

307. Owls have been noticed for an extraordinary
attachment to their young. Whether, however, it exceeds
that of other birds or animals may be very difficult to
say, but they will certainly visit and feed them long
after they have been separated from the nest. Some
young owls which had been so far tamed as to take food
from the hand, were observed to lose all their familiarity
on being hung out during the night, in consequence of
several visits from the parent birds, who fed them with
as much care and attention as if they had been with
them without interruption.

308. Another instance in point was witnessed by a
Swedish gentleman, who resided several years on a farm
near a steep mountain, on the summit of which two
eagle owls had built their nest. One day in the month
of July, a young bird having quitted the nest was caught
by the servants. This bird was, considering the season

of the year, well feathered, but the down appeared here
and there between those feathers which had not yet
attained their full growth. After it was caught, it was
shut up in a large hen-coop, when to his surprise on the
following morning a fine young partridge was found
lying dead before the door of the coop. It was immediately concluded that this provision had been
brought there by the old owls, which no doubt had been
making search in the night-time for their lost young
one, and such was indeed the fact, for night after night
for fourteen days was this same mark of attention repeated. The game which the old ones carried to it
consisted chiefly of young partridges, for the most
part newly killed, but sometimes a little spoiled. It
was supposed that the spoiled flesh had already been
some time in the nest of the old ones, and that they had
brought it merely because they had no better provision
at the time. The gentleman and his servant watched
several nights in order that they might observe, through
a window, when and how this supply was brought, but
in vain, for it appeared that the owls, which are very
quick-sighted, had discovered the moment when the
window was not watched, as food was found to be
placed before the coop on these very nights. In the
month of August, the attention on the part of the old
birds ceased, but it should be observed that this was
about the usual period when all birds of prey abandon
their young to their own exertions, and usually drive
them off to shift for themselves in distant haunts.

# THE FLYCATCHER.

—•❧❦•—

The cold ungenial north suits not this bird,
And so he journeys to a land where bowers
Are ever green, to visit us again.

309. The flycatcher builds every year in the vines
which grow on the walls of my house. A pair of these
little birds had one year placed their nest on a bough,
in a shady lime, perhaps not being aware of the inconvenience which followed; but a hot sunny season
coming, before the brood was half fledged the reflection
of the wall became insupportable, and must inevitably
have destroyed the tender young, had not affection suggested an expedient, and prompted the parent birds to
hover over the nest all the hotter hours, while with
wings expanded, and mouths gasping for breath, they
screened off the heat from their suffering offspring.

# THE WILLOW-WREN.

———••✦✦✦••———

Come, fairy bird, and my sheltering trees
Shall shield thy wing from the ruffling breeze.

310. A further instance I once saw of noble sagacity
in a willow wren, which had built in a bank of my field.
This bird, a friend and myself had observed as she sat
in her nest, but were particularly careful not to disturb
her, though we saw she eyed us with some degree of
jealousy. Some days after as we passed that way, we
were desirous of remarking how this brood went on;
but no nest could be found, till I happened to take up a
bundle of long green moss, as it were carelessly thrown
over the nest, in order to dodge the eye of any imper-
tinent intruder.

# THE CROW.

———•﹗✖﹗•﹢——

"There are certain kinds of intellectual power—of what, in men, at least, is commonly called reason—common, to a certain extent, to man and to some of the lower orders of creation."
SALAD FOR THE SOCIAL.

311. THE common crow is very easily tamed, and is strongly attached to the person who brings him up. I kept one for two years and a half. It flew round about the neighbourhood and roosted every night on the trees of my shrubbery. At whatever distance he was, as soon as he heard my voice, he immediately came to me. He was very fond of being caressed. His memory was astonishing. One Monday morning, after being satiated with food, he picked up a mole which was lying in the orchard, and hopped with it into the garden. I kept out of his sight, as he seldom concealed anything when he thought you observed him. He covered it so nicely with earth, that upon the most diligent search I could not discover where he had put it. As his wings had been cut to prevent him from flying over the wall into the garden, he made many a fruitless attempt during the week to get in at the door. On Saturday evening, however it had been left open, I saw him hop to the very spot where the mole had been so

long hid, and to my surprise he came out with it in the twinkling of an eye.

312. In the spring of 1791, a pair of crows made their nest on a tree, of which there are several planted round Mr. ———'s garden; and in his morning walks he had often been amused by witnessing furious combats between them and a cat. One morning the battle raged more fiercely than usual, till at last the cat gave way, and took shelter under a hedge, as if to wait a more favourable opportunity of retreating to the house. The crows continued for a short time to make a threatening noise; but perceiving that on the ground they could do nothing more than threaten, one of them lifted a stone from the middle of the garden, and perched with it on a tree planted in the hedge, where she sat watching the motion of the enemy of her young. As she crept along under the hedge, the crow accompanied her by flying from branch to branch, and from tree to tree; and when at last puss ventured to quit her hiding place, the crow leaving the trees, and hovering over her in the air, let the stone drop from on high on her back. That the crow on this occasion reasoned, is self-evident; and it seems to be little less evident that the ideas employed in her reasoning were enlarged beyond those which she had received from her senses. By her senses, she may have perceived that the shell of a fish is broken by a fall; but could her senses inform her that a cat would be wounded or driven off the field by the fall of a stone? No. From the effect of the one fall preserved in her memory, she must have inferred the other by the power of reasoning. (I give this *cum grano salis.*)

s

# THE ROBIN.

—••+✖+••—

Thou art the bird whom man loves best,
The pious bird with the scarlet breast,
   Our little English Robin ;
The bird that comes about our doors,
   When autumn winds are sobbing.
Thou art the Peter of Norway boors,
   Their Thomas in Finland,
   And Russia far inland,
The bird who by some name or other
All men who know thee call thee brother.—Wordsworth.

313. A LADY has furnished me with the following
striking instance of maternal affection in a red-breast
that had built in some ivy against a wall in a garden at
Whitburn, near Sunderland, in April 1839. The bird
was sitting upon four eggs, when the gardener one day
trimmed the ivy so close with his shears, as almost to
destroy the nest; in consequence of which the eggs
were precipitated to the ground. They lay there till
observed by the lady shortly afterwards, who was
attracted to the spot by the plaintive cries of the parent
bird. It was at first thought that to restore them to
the nest would prove useless. The attempt, however,
was made ; the eggs, which were nearly cold, were
picked up, and placed back again in the nest, after it
had been repaired and put together again as well as was
possible. They had not been returned to their former
situation five minutes, when the bird came, and again
took charge of them, and in two days they were hatched ;

the infant brood being from that time, of course, objects
of daily interest and observation. Great was the dismay of the lady, some days afterwards, at finding all
the little ones upon the ground, stiff and cold, having
fallen through a fracture in the patched nest which was
not sufficiently strong to keep them together. She
took them up, and perceiving a slight movement in one
of them, carried them into the house, where, partly by
the warmth of the hand, and partly by the influence of
the fire to which they were held, they all gradually
recovered. They were then again placed in the nest,
which was further patched with a piece of drugget,
fastened into the fracture through which they had
fallen. They were doomed, however, to go through
more trials; for it happened, some nights after there
was a heavy rain, which so completely soaked the nest,
and the drugget which had been placed in it as a lining,
that the young ones were found the following morning
almost drowned, and to appearance lifeless. They were
again brought to the fire, and thoroughly dried. After
which, they were placed in the empty nest of another
bird that was substituted for the old one, and fixed in
a currant bush a few yards from the wall where the ivy
was. The young ones, which were half-fledged when
they got this wetting, still continued to receive the
attentions of their parents, and in due time they were
all safely reared, and flew away. It is stated that it was
very curious to observe the familiarity of the old birds
during the whole course of these proceedings: they
always sat close by, and never seemed the least alarmed
at the liberties taken with their progeny

# THE GOOSE.

····ː❋ː··─

Evil, like us, they shun, and covet good;
Abhor the poison, and secure the food.
Like us they love or hate; like us they know
To greet the friend, or grapple with the foe.
With seeming thought their actions they intend,
And use the means proportioned to the end;
Then vainly the philosopher avers
That reason guides our heads and instinct theirs.
How can we justly different answers frame,
When the effects entirely are the same?
Instinct and reason how can we divide?
'Tis the fool's ignorance and the pedant's pride.—PRIOR.

314. WITHOUT speaking of the attention due to the
goose for its pecuniary worth, beyond this, it has qualities, we might almost say, of the mind, of a very singular
character; we mean the unaccountable constancy and
affection which it has been known to show, not only to
its own species and to other birds and animals, but more
particularly to man ; and it is not improbable that these
qualities, which, as we shall soon show, were known to
the ancients, might have rendered it an object of high
esteem, and in some cases sacred ; as, for instance, it
was to Juno, the queen of their idol gods.  In addition
to which it has other qualifications, proving the fallacy
of the proverbial libel, " As silly as a goose."  Thus its
watchfulness at night time has always been noted ; and

it certainly is endowed with a strong organ of self-pre-
servation, for, as has been well observed, you may drive
over cat, dog, hen, pig, or even pigeons, but few, if any,
can record an instance of driving over a tame goose;
and as for wild-geese, there is no animal, biped or quadruped, so difficult to deceive or approach, their sense of
hearing, seeing, and smelling, being so exceedingly
acute; independent of which they seem to act in so
organised and cautious a manner when feeding or roost-
ing, as to defy all danger. Sportsmen could give
instances without number of their utmost skill being of
no avail in attempting to approach these birds; either
a careless step on a piece of gravel, or an eddy of wind,
however light, or letting them perceive the smallest
portion of their persons, has rendered useless whole
hours of manœuvering.

315. Of its attachment to the human race, says Bishop
Stanley, Pliny, an ancient Roman writer, gives several
instances: one only we select, as closely resembling
that with which we shall conclude.—A person named
Lacydes, a philosopher, had a goose which took so
strong a fancy to him, that it would never willingly
leave him, by day or night. Wherever he went the
goose was his companion; if he went abroad and walked
in the public streets, the bird followed him; and in his
own house, always forced itself into his presence. The
philosopher, struck with this constant and strange
attachment, seems to have considered it as in some way
connected with religious feelings; and accordingly,
when at last it died, he was at the expense of bestowing
upon it a magnificent funeral.

316. Our next instance occurred in Scotland. A goose a year old, formed a similar attachment to a person in Elgin, and would follow him any distance, even through the crowd and bustle of the main street. One day, when going down the street, its master went into a hair-dresser's shop to be shaved, whereupon the bird waited patiently till the operation was finished, and then accompanied him to the house of a friend; after which it proceeded home with him. Change of dress seemed to make no difference in the bird's power of distinguishing its master, for in whatever dress he appeared, the goose recognised him; and whenever he spoke, it responded with a cry expressive of satisfaction.

317. Another similar case is on record in Germany. An aged blind woman, who probably might have been in the habit of feeding it, used to be led every Sunday to church by a gander, taking hold of her gown with his bill. When she had seated herself, it retired to graze in the churchyard till she came out again, when it led her home. One day, the clergyman called at her house, and expressing his surprise to her daughter, that her mother should venture abroad; she replied, "Oh, sir, we are not afraid of trusting her out of sight, for the gander is with her."

318. The Bishop continues, "We frankly own that so strange and improbable as the above stories appear, we should neither have inserted, or paid the slightest attention to them, had we not the following testimony to their credibility, for the accuracy of which we can readily vouch; and deeply do we regret that a better fate did not await so extraordinary a bird, which

under more intelligent observers, might have afforded opportunities of ascertaining the extent of so unusual a developement of affection.—A farmer in Cheshire possessed a flock of geese, one of which, at the end of about three years, without any apparent cause, began to show a peculiar partiality for its master. It first appeared on the bird's quitting its companions in the farm-yard or pond, and stalking after him. These symptoms became daily stronger, and in a short time wherever the farmer went, whether to the mill, or the blacksmith's shop, or through the bustling streets of a neighbouring manufacturing town, the goose was at his heels: so perseveringly did it follow his steps, that if he wished to go out alone, he was under the necessity of fastening up the bird. The farmer was in the habit of holding his own plough, and on these occasions, the goose as regularly passed the day in the ploughing field, walking sedately, not with the usual waddling pace of its fellow geese, but with a firm step, head erected, and neck erect, a short way before him, in the line of the furrows, frequently turning round and fixing its eyes intently upon him. When the length of one furrow was accomplished, and the plough turned, the goose, without losing its step, adroitly wheeled about, and thus continued its attendance till the leaving, and then followed its master home; and if permitted, would mount upon his lap as he sat by the fire after dark, showing the strongest signs of affection, and nestling its head in his bosom, and preening the hair of his head with its beak, as it was wont to do its own feathers. Sometimes the farmer would go out shooting, and no

sooner had he shouldered his gun, than his companion
was at his post, following him as before, in spite of
every obstacle, " getting over," to use the man's own
words, " the fences as well as I could myself."  All this,
it should be observed, continued not only without any
encouragement on the part of the farmer, but even in
spite of long discouragement on his part.  How long it
would have continued, or to what extent, we lament to
add, he effectually precluded the world from knowing ;
for with an unpardonable inattention to so truly a wonderful ease, in addition to an equally unpardonable
superstitious fear, he took it into his head that the
mysterious affection of the goose foreboded some evil,
and in a moment of alarm, he killed the faithful bird.

THE END.

COULTAS, PRINTER, HIGH-OUSEGATE, YORK.

www.ingramcontent.com/pod-product-compliance
Lightning Source LLC
Chambersburg PA
CBHW020503270326

*9 7 8 3 7 4 4 7 6 7 9 5 8 *